DEDICATION

To Rosemary Cullen Owens for turning me towards the diaries and for re-establishing (with others) the Irish Section of the Women's International League for Peace and Freedom, which would have delighted Lucy.

ACKNOWLEDGEMENTS

I acknowledge with gratitude the help of the following: Annelies Becker, Elizabeth Bell, Campbell Boyd, Francis Devine and Jennie Hunter of the Irish Labour History Museum; Richard Harrison, Gráinne Healy, Daphne Huggard, Frank Jones, Michael Kenny of the National Museum, Sean O'Criadain, Rosemary Cullen Owens, Elsa Peile, Ailbhe Smyth, Eva Swanton, Richard and Clare Swanton, Stella Webb, Jonathan and Sylvia Wigham and Billy and Meta Wilson.

The poem 'Wind' from *The Hawk in the Rain* is quoted by kind permission of Ted Hughes.

I could not have attempted this venture without the constant advice and technical assistance of Trevor McCay-Morrissey, the guidance and encouragement of Attic Press, and the unending patience of my family.

E‌

and
Lucy Olive Kingston

ased on Personal Diaries, 1883–1969

Daisy Lawrenson Swanton

Attic Press
DUBLIN

First published in Ireland in 1994 by
Attic Press
4 Upper Mount Street
Dublin 2

A catalogue record for this title is available from the British Library

ISBN 1-855940-493

The moral right of Daisy Lawrenson Swanton to be identified as the author of this work is asserted.

Cover Design: Syd Bluett
Origination: Verbatim Typesetting and Design
Printing: Guernsey Press Co Ltd.

This book is published with the assistance of The Arts Council/An Chomhairle Ealaíon.

CONTENTS

FOREWORD

In relating the stories of my grandmother's and mother's lives, based upon their voluminous diaries from 1883 to 1969 (and other family papers), I wish to show how 'women's issues' were a living concern for many women from the earliest years of this century.

My own sense of gratitude leads me to quote George Eliot's comment on Dorothea Brooke in *Middlemarch:* 'But the effect of her being on those around her was incalculably diffusive: for the growing good of the world is partly dependent on unhistoric acts; and that things are not so ill with you and me as they might have been, is half owing to the number who lived faithfully a hidden life, and rest in unvisited tombs'.

In choosing the title *Emerging from the Shadow,* I also wish to show how my grandmother emerged from an unhappy and restricted life into one in which she took her own decisions and imbued her four daughters with ambition and idealism.

Her youngest daughter Lucy had a much happier and more fulfilled life and enjoyed working for many causes. However, she lived through many 'shadows': the struggle for equality and recognition for women, international wars and civil strife, the growing nuclear threat, the pain of bereavements and the effort to discern spiritual truth. Her poem 'Song' (undated) was written quite early in her life but seems prophetic and a suitable finale.

D. L. S.
Cobh, County Cork 1993

PART 1

Sarah Anne Lawrenson

PROLOGUE

This tale begins with the life of Sarah Anne Hopkins in County Wicklow. Before embarking on her own story, let us look back to the early life of some of the women who preceded her.

In 1814 a young girl, the youngest of a family of fourteen, living in Drinagh, County Carlow, began and completed a sampler. As was customary, she carefully worked the alphabet and then moved to the verses:

Virtue's the Chiefest Beauty of the Mind
The Noblest Ornament of Human Kind
Virtue's our Safeguard and our guiding Star
That stirs up Reason when our Senses err.

Since gentle Sleep has chas'd away
The painful Toils of Yesterday
Now let me vig'rous rise
For Study chearfully prepare
And follow with industrious Care
The Means to make me wise.

> Charlotte Keppel her Work Septr 1814

An elder sister of Charlotte's wrote this letter:

> Rathrush February 1827

Dearest John,
I hope you will not attribute my long silence to my neglect: it proceeded from want of time, as I was going from home with my cousin Hopkins at the same time when I received your letter. As you required an answer I therefore let you know that I could have no objection; however if my parents be satisfied, I am also well pleased.

> Yours with best wishes,
> Sarah Keppel

The 'Dearest John' was John Salter of Ballingowan, County Carlow. He and Sarah married and had five children, Anna, Peter, Jane, Alicia and Susan. When Susan was only four, her mother died. The girls were sent to Keppel relatives and Peter went as weekly boarder to Reverend Jamieson, Carlow. Within a few years John Salter proposed to Charlotte Keppel, who had been a bridesmaid at his first wedding. When they married, his three younger daughters were reunited with their father. Anna, the eldest, remained with George Keppel and his wife until she married William Young of Ballygalduff. John and Charlotte Salter had two children, William and Sarah. They left Ballingowan and lived in Knocknegan, County Carlow.

When Sarah, his youngest child, was about three, John contracted typhus fever and died. His son Peter, then about sixteen, got on very well with his step-mother Charlotte, who was said to have been very wise, so she must have heeded the sentiments of her 1814 sampler. They ran the farm together and prospered, also buying in three or four outlying farms, and were looked upon as among the largest landowners in County Carlow. However, when her daughter Sarah was about eleven, Charlotte died.

Peter was very disturbed by her death. He occasioned great surprise by proposing to another of the Drinagh Keppel family, Jane Lee, who was a niece of his step-mother. She was considerably older than Peter, and said to be silly, extravagant and useless. The story was told that at their wedding she behaved in such a silly fashion that Peter said to his sister, 'For God's sake, Susan, take her out of my sight'. They lived at Jane's mother's house for the first year and returned to Knocknegan only so that their son would be born there.

During the same year (about 1854) three of John and Sarah Salter's daughters each married a Hopkins, which seems scarcely credible. As Sarah Keppel had mentioned in her acceptance of her proposal, there was already a cousinship with the Hopkins family, so a family tree would be very complicated. Jane married Matthew Hopkins, Alicia married William Hopkins and Susan married Edward Hopkins and went to live at Stratnakelly, the old Hopkins home near Shillelagh, County Wicklow.

Peter Salter's previous industry was now a thing of the past. To drown the sorrows caused by his unwise marriage, he turned to drink, and the running of the farm fell upon John and Charlotte's children, William and Sarah, he managing the farm and she the dairy. Sarah Salter was very hardworking and energetic, driving Peter's two daughters to boarding school in Carlow each Monday and collecting them again each Saturday. She was very attached to her half-sister Susan Hopkins and frequently would tie her night things onto her pony and ride over to Stratnakelly to spend the night, returning in the morning to attend to her dairy at Knocknegan.

Her brother married Elizabeth Burland but Peter was very much against his half-sister Sarah marrying because she was so useful to him. She had met yet another Hopkins (William of Ballybitt) but Peter raised the objection that she would be the first in their family to marry into trade. She and William Hopkins were engaged for some years but finally she prevailed upon Peter to agree to her wedding in 1869. Some years later she and William lived in a lovely house with gardens bordering the Dargle River outside Bray, County Wicklow, called La Vallée. The frowned-upon 'trade' was that of watchmaker, silversmith and jeweller in the well-known firm of Hopkins and Hopkins on the corner of Sackville Street and Eden Quay in Dublin.

CHAPTER ONE
1855–1882

On the eighth day of May, 1855, Edward Hopkins and his wife Susan, formerly Salter, celebrated the birth of their first child, Sarah Anne. They lived at Stratnakelly, near Shillelagh in south County Wicklow, in a medium-sized Victorian house on a gently rolling hillside. Seven other children followed: John (mildly mentally handicapped), William, Robert, Jane, Thomas, Joseph and Elizabeth.

So began the life of a woman who, though born into a middle-class Protestant rural family, was to experience tragedies and face many hard decisions in her life. She would eventually live in many different houses, taking on the sole responsibility of parenthood for her own surviving children at a time when opportunities for financial independence for women were few and those that did exist demanded hard work and perseverance. These were the abiding qualities of Sarah Anne Hopkins Lawrenson until the end of her life in 1928.

The Hopkins children had one another for company and had many friends and relations in the general area of Shillelagh and also in County Carlow, as their mother's family home was Knocknegan, near Tullow. They attended the local Protestant school and also Sunday School, where they were taught Bible stories, prayers and hymns. There were many other church activities such as missionary and temperance meetings where they met their neighbours, most of whom were members of the Church of Ireland.

It was a farming community so the children were accustomed to the care of animals from an early age. The girls also started learning needlework when very young. It was customary to teach a variety of embroidery stitches by reproducing the alphabet and then some suitable verse

9

or prayer on a strong piece of material, which was termed a sampler. A typical sampler of the period stitched by Sarah Anne shows the alphabet in block capitals followed by:

Praise God, from whom all blessings flow
Praise him all creatures here below
Praise him above ye heavenly host,
Praise father, son and holy ghost.

Sarah Hopkins her sampler wrought
May virtue guide her in her thought
And when to heaven she soars away
May angels guard her on her way.

The date is not decipherable, but she was probably about ten at the time. The first 's' in blessings is similar to an 'f', which was also the custom in legal documents whenever a double 's' occurred. The sampler is bordered by embroidered pink rosettes and leaves and, although now the worse for wear, is a touching example of Sarah Anne's early lessons in industry and piety.

As Sarah Anne became an adolescent, she was taught much more extensive needlework and also music, as she played the piano and harmonium. She loved to sing hymns, and developed a love of reading which remained with her all her life.

As well as various church functions, she and her siblings accompanied their father to the various horse fairs and cattle shows held at centres throughout the County of Wicklow, sometimes in Wicklow town and also in Rathdrum and Glenealy. Walking in all weathers would have been taken for granted, but she was also taught to manage a pony and trap and she learned to play tennis. Holidays were rare during Victorian times, especially among the hard-working farming communities, but visits for short or long periods to other family homes were much enjoyed. When William Hopkins and Sarah Salter of

Knocknegan married in 1869, Sarah Salter had ten bridesmaids, mostly children. Two of these children were Sarah Anne and Janie Hopkins from Stratnakelly. Sarah Anne was then fourteen and Janie seven. Such were the convolutions of the family relationships that the bridegroom was first cousin to the Stratnakelly girls and the bride was their aunt.

As the girls grew older, they were taught to cook, to churn and to keep basic accounts. All these skills stood Sarah Anne in good stead in her later life. There was a great deal of work in a household which bought only basic foodstuffs and the girls all made their own clothes. There were usually daily maids employed who would have been daughters of farm labourers living in the vicinity. These maids were probably the only close contact Sarah Anne would have had with Catholics, as social contacts seem to have been very much centred on the local Church of Ireland.

When Edward Hopkins died in August 1880, his widow and children continued to live at Stratnakelly and Tom ran the farm. Later both Joseph and Robert Hopkins emigrated to Australia after some unexplained financial difficulties. There was a good deal of emigration of younger sons in their circle; it seemed to be the alternative then to splitting up family farms. It was, of course, customary for daughters to remain at home unless they married. Sarah Anne was the first of her family to marry, at the age of twenty-nine. Her husband was Robert Lawrenson.

From the census figures in 1881, it appears that almost 80 per cent of the population of County Wicklow was Roman Catholic and only just over 18 per cent members of the Church of Ireland. The majority of the Protestants were either middle-class farmers and shopkeepers, or upper-class landowners. Figures from a survey in 1876 show that 66 per cent of the land in Ireland was owned by fewer than two thousand landowners with estates in excess of two thousand acres. In effect only 800 landlords owned half the country. This gross imbalance caused much unrest and was gradually redressed after the 1881 Land Act, but County Wicklow still contained many large estates such as Avondale at Avoca, owned by the Parnell family.

A prominent feature of Shillelagh was the Earl of FitzWilliam's great house and woods at Coolattin. This estate comprised four thousand acres in County Wicklow and a slate quarry near Carnew. At one time the estate ran a paint factory. Stewards or agents and under-agents were responsible for farm management and the collection of rents from tenant farmers on the estate. Ralph Lawrenson was an under-agent and he and his family lived in a large house called Ballykelly about six miles from Stratnakelly. Rent collection was a hazardous occupation before the 1881 Land Act and two armed guards travelled round with him on occasions, but he was a well-respected and fair-minded man. When he died suddenly in 1882, an eighteen-foot-high of obelisk of pink polished granite was erected to his memory by public subscription and can still be seen near Shillelagh Church of Ireland.

CHAPTER TWO
1883–1885

Sarah Anne's life was busy, sheltered and unsophisticated, her only opportunities for meeting people outside the wider family circle occurring either through church contacts or farming occasions. She would have known Robert Lawrenson from his visits to his elder brother Ralph at Ballykelly, and when she was twenty-eight they became engaged at a horse fair at Wicklow. They married six months later on 23 October 1883 at Mullinacuffe Church, near Stratnakelly, and went to live at Robert's home Ballinakill, near Glenealy.

Ballinakill was a pleasant, comfortable early-Victorian house which had been left to Robert under the terms of his father's will. Robert was the third son, but his older brothers Ralph and John were already provided for, so the farm and lands were bequeathed to Robert with the proviso that he would fully support Anne Lawrenson, his mother, as long as she wished to remain at Ballinakill. In addition, Robert was to support his four sisters Jane, Sarah, Elizabeth and Anne until they married, on which occasion each was to receive a dowry of two hundred pounds. This will was dated 30 April 1869 and came into effect on Robert's father's death on 16 July 1874.

This meant that not only had Sarah Anne to take up a new life as a married woman (with, one can assume, no sex education of any sort), but she also had to come to terms with living with her mother-in-law and four adult sisters-in-law, all of whom had full rights of residence and support in their family home. Robert was fifteen years her senior but they would seem to have been very well-matched in their background and interests and they undoubtedly loved one another. It is therefore difficult to understand why Sarah Anne was so resented by the

Lawrenson women throughout her nine years at Ballinakill but resented she was. This caused her great misery through the years.

One feels particularly for her during her stressful first year. She was only a few months married when her mother became ill and died at Stratnakelly and Sarah Anne, as the eldest, was needed at home, so she returned to help her family for a few months.

The railway system then known as the Dublin, Wicklow and Wexford Railway was of great benefit to Sarah Anne for keeping in touch with her family. In 1865 the line between Rathdrum and Arklow had been extended by a sixteen-and-a-half mile branch from Woodenbridge Junction westwards to Shillelagh. This served stations at Aughrim, Ballinglen, Tinahely and Shillelagh with two trains each way daily until 1902, when the number of trains was increased to five.

Sarah Anne returned by train to Ballinakill in April 1884 and was met by Robert. Next day they had early dinner and she went out with him branding lambs. The following day she drove him to Glenealy for the cattle show and, as this was the first night he was away from her at Ballinakill, her sister-in-law Anne slept with her. Anne was the most friendly of the Lawrenson women and was reasonably companionable, but Sarah Anne had great difficulty with her namesake Sarah Lawrenson who seemed to be a most unbalanced person.

On 30 April, poor Sarah Anne noted in her diary that she felt angry and unhappy. 'Robert went early to Rathdrum and I spent my day crying like a baby.' In June she commented that, 'Things were going wrong and I had a good cry.' She was six months pregnant and suffering from neuralgia. On 23 June, she noted that she was eight months married and that she was a little vexed that Anne went with Robert to the fair at Wicklow and was out all day. Her confinement to the home with every pregnancy was an aspect of her role as mother and wife which Sarah

Anne never quite came to terms with, although it would have been normal for women of her class at this time.

Sarah Anne decided that her first child would be born at Stratnakelly and went there about the middle of September, 1884. Her entry for 25 September was: 'A dreadful day on me. Kidd (doctor) here all day. Baby born about 9.30 p.m. A fine fellow, Thank Mercy.'

It is interesting to note her extreme reticence throughout all her childbearing years. The only inkling of each pregnancy is an entry about two or three months before the expected date: 'Start little things', presumably baby clothes. There was no ante-natal care, nurse and doctor appeared to be booked about a fortnight before the confinement date, Sarah always referred to being 'ill' or 'laid up' rather than to being in labour and post-natal care ended a few days after the birth.

She returned to Ballinakill, Robert having called to collect her. On 16 November her diary entry was: 'In the evening got my little pet baptised.' He was usually called Ralphie. She took entire charge of the baby herself and referred to occupations such as quilting, singing hymns, reading about 'Barnardos' and a book on Pompeii. Thomas Barnardo was born in Dublin and began to work with homeless children in the east end of London while he was engaged in medical studies at London Hospital. He wrote articles on his work in an evangelical paper called *The Christian* which may have been what Sarah Anne was reading. He later established Boys' Homes and Cottage Homes for Girls and enabled some children to emigrate to Canada.

There must have been much confusion within the family regarding names, as Sarah Anne and her two sisters had the same names as Robert's sisters. This may have led Robert and Sarah Anne to break new ground with their six children as they were called Ralph, Ethel, Elsie, Winifred, Theodora and Lucy.

Sarah Anne frequently mentioned churning and fruit-picking, as well as much sewing, including making Robert's shirts. Her expenditure on clothes was very modest, judging by the following account:

Clothes for self since marriage
Nov. 1883
1 pr. strong boots 6/6

Feb. 1884
2 aprons 2/-; 1 pr. stockings 1/6d; 3/6
Bonnet 6/9; Crape etc. 10/10; 17/7.

May
Hat 1/7; Stockings 10d.; Dolman 19/6; £1/1/11
Tennis shoes 3/6; Print dress 6/2; 9/8.

August
Apron 9d; Stays 7/6; 8/3.

November
Trimming jacket and apron 5/2. Total till Christmas '84
£3/12/7

The total shown for 1885 was £3/2/0 and for 1886 was £1/1/11.

During this time Sarah wrote many letters and was always eager to receive post, as she kept in close touch with her sisters Janie and Lizzie. The postal service was very quick and reliable but letters had to be collected from the nearest post office. Sarah's brother Tom frequently visited Ballinakill on his way to or from fairs.

Occasionally Sarah Anne was able to attend her local church services, visit neighbours and go to missionary and temperance meetings. The missionary meetings included descriptions of the evangelising work undertaken in Africa, China and Japan, and sales of work were organised to raise funds. Temperance meetings usually included stern warnings about the evils of over-indulgence in alcohol.

In April Sarah listed in her diary 'Hints to a Mother' which were on how to deal with diarrhoea, costiveness, thrush, croup, measles, scarlet fever and indigestion, the last being a recipe:

1/2 lb. figs, 1/2 lb. raisins, 1 oz. fine senna.

Mix together and chop fine.

Put all in jar and cover with spirits. Tie down close. Take a piece the size of a walnut every morning fasting.

This sounds more like a cure for constipation than indigestion. Sarah Anne also noted during this month that she had had a long talk with her sisters-in-law about their prospects.

By August she was trying to take herself in hand. 'I have resolved this day with God's help to rise before 6 o'c. and to read less and be more industrious.' On 19 August she went to a missionary meeting and magic lantern lecture on Japan. A magic lantern was very popular as a means of illustrating lectures. It consisted of a metal box in which a light from a lamp passed through a condensing lens, then through a partly transparent picture or slide, then out through another lens to form an enlarged image of the picture on a distant white screen. She sent to Stratnakelly for her piano which was delivered with a 'wicked letter' from her sister Lizzie. Presumably Lizzie resented Sarah Anne's right as elder sister to the piano but she later wrote to apologise.

Sarah Anne's entry for 23 October 1885 was: 'Two years married to-day. Wet and miserable. The Mother insulted me about Mrs Pasco (a friend Sarah Anne had visited recently in Wicklow). Cried nearly all day.'

This appears to confirm that her mother-in-law regarded Sarah Anne and her friends as not being of the same class as the Lawrensons, which have been at the root of her constant disapproval of her daughter-in-law. A week later 'Sarah cross and I rebelled, crying like a fool and very miserable. Robert not home till late. Everything unpleasant.' Next day: 'Complaining to Robert of which I'm sorry now.' By November 29: 'Stayed in reading night and day. Lonely and cross. Baby very uneasy at night.' and next day: 'Resolved to-day with God's help to be more firm and strongminded, both with baby and everything else.'

Things were increasingly difficult for Sarah Anne during December and she was six months pregnant again, but she did seem to be gradually becoming more assertive. Every few days she made resolutions: 'Resolved to-day by God's help to be more self-denying in regard to food etc. Also more economical about my time.' 'Resolved to be more guarded both about private and family matters.' 'Very angry with the Gran and discontented with everything. Heaven forgive me.' 'Vexed and lonely. Crying as usual.' 'Robert at a great hunt in White Cross roads. Very cross about seeing so little of Robert.' 'Rowing at Robert about my position here early in the morning. Vexed with myself later.' 'The last of old year. I thank God for all his mercies to me and all I love during this year, and I pray that if we are spared thro' another year, we may live more for Him, and less for ourselves.'

These resolutions show how hard Sarah Anne was finding sharing the house with her in-laws, and also indicate the strains this situation placed, from time to time, on her marriage and family life.

However, we can also see from her resolutions that she is trying to modify her outspoken nature and habits to reduce the number of open confrontations. This in turn would mean less draining of her energy expended upsetting domestic rows.

CHAPTER 3
1886–1892

In January 1886 there were heavy snowfalls, then a thaw and it was very wet, so Sarah Anne was housebound and worried about Robert looking badly. On 1 March there was a dreadful snowstorm: 'Robert intended going to funeral but could not. Place in great slop.' Once again Sarah: 'Resolved by God's help to devote a little time every morning to pray for Robert and baby.' 'Awoke in a vex and cried all day. Never spent a much worse Sunday. From fire to bed and back.' Only two days before her second baby was born she overheard 'usual unpleasant talk about Robert's foolish marriage' among her in-laws.

On 20 March she sent for her sister Janie who came that evening by the last train. Susan Ethel was born and Sarah Anne got through the birth well but the baby was very weak and ill. It must have helped Sarah Anne to have her own sister with her and she noted a few days later that she and Janie both had a good cry. However, Janie left again on 1 April, and Sarah Anne was lonely, cross and discontented and 'vexed with the Grannie.'

Towards the end of May she got to church for the first time since January. By June she noted: 'Anne giving out the pay for fear of large family. Annoyed.' Sarah Anne's annoyance is surely understandable, as she had no desire for such frequent pregnancies herself and felt this as fresh unfair criticism. On 13 June the baby Ethel was baptised and later vaccinated, but she was very sick by the end of the month.

There are frequent references during these years to the presence of Sam, her brother-in-law. He drove the trap, went to social functions and was generally a part of the household but did not appear to do much work. He heard from a neighbour an enthusiastic account of Manitoba,

Canada, and after this there was some talk of his emigrating. Sarah Anne braced herself to talk to him about it but finally his favourite sister Lizzie did so, and he must have then made plans.

One can gather that Sarah Anne continued to resent the number of outings that Anne was free to take with Robert while hers were curtailed by the children. However, there was suddenly some mention of visits from Robert Alford. By August he had proposed to Anne and had been accepted, and there was a rare comment from Sarah Anne about pleasant days. However, by 14 August: 'Gran and Sarah most troublesome' and 'Lizzie and I have a long talk of affairs'—presumably rearranging domestic duties. On 1 September, 'Anne, Ralphie and I drove to Rathdrum. Anne buying calico for trousseau.'

A week later she noted: 'Ralphie has rash like measles —not well. Doctor pays second visit. Sam's last Sunday with us, poor fellow.' A later entry was: 'Sam left for Canada. Jane and Anne at loggerheads about Alford.'

On 8 November: 'Anne's last day. Great cleaning up for wedding. Piano moved to drawingroom.' Next day: 'Anne's wedding day which I won't easily forget. Happy pair left at 5 p.m.' Perhaps Sarah Anne's grim tone was because she usually felt slighted when there were social occasions at Ballinakill, as her mother-in-law was always the hostess, rather than Sarah Anne.

On 16 November, her sister Lizzie surprised her by walking in from Rathdrum after dark. She came intending to take Ralphie back to Stratnakelly. A week later: 'Robert drove Lizzie and Ralphie to 11.30 train. Poor Ralphie, the first night he was ever away from me.' Ralphie was taken by his aunts to visit various family homes for the next fortnight, presumably with the intention of giving Sarah Anne a little break. However, on 12 December her entry was: 'Robert and I at church. So busy and tired it did not seem like Sunday.' Next day she was busy churning, but feeling tired and sick (which meant that she was pregnant again). On 16 December she heard that Ralphie was poorly and wrote to Janie.

The next day a telegram from one of her brothers about family business obliged her and Robert to leave hastily by train for Dublin where there were consultations and possibly revelations of financial trouble—she does not elaborate, just mentions dreadful scenes. They got home by the last train on 18 December, but next day: 'Gran outrageous. Heard Ralphie poorly. Decided to go.' She went to Stratnakelly by first train on 20 December, and was surprised to see Ralphie so low: 'He, Janie and I slept in big room. Last time for me ever to sleep with him. Heaven help me.'

It would seem that one of the few outings since their marriage for Sarah Anne and Robert, alone, was to be marred by a tragedy of great proportions—the death of their beloved son Ralphie.

There was no diary entry for three months and one can only piece together the tragedy from later entries on anniversaries. Ralphie, aged two years and three months, died on 26 December 1886, about a week after Sarah Anne reached him. The cause of his death is given as 'water in the brain three weeks' and then the words 'tubercular meningitis twenty days certified'. On 15 February 1887, Ethel died at eleven months of 'acute tubercular meningitis twenty-two days certified'. This second death was at Stratnakelly where Sarah Anne had probably been since Ralphie's death. She was heartbroken at this double loss and for the rest of her life never failed to mention the successive birthdays of Ralphie and the age he would have been.

She resumed her diary in March. Entries show her looking after a pet lamb, paying visits with and without Robert and trying to put her life together again. However, on 27 March she noted: 'Great row with Sarah— everything unpleasant' so nothing much had changed. She commented on the bitterly cold weather that Easter.

On 16 April she wrote: 'Had a good cry for my poor children. Commenced sewing for third baby with very different feelings from the others.' In June: 'Sickish. Lazy day reading *Jane Eyre*. Dreadfully hot. Greatly tormented by bad dreams.'

In July the family were shocked to hear news that Sam had died in Canada. 'Great grief and everything unpleasant.' Sarah Anne does not indicate what happened to him, but in November his box was delivered. This was deeply upsetting for the family again, especially for his sister Lizzie who was very attached to him.

Sarah Anne was nearing the end of her third pregnancy on 6 August , and yet: 'Sarah and I great row. Struck me. In dumps all day.'

On 8 August, Sarah Anne's diary note was: 'Awoke poorly at 4.30. I pray to God to bring me safely thro' this trial. Sent telegram for Janie and for Mrs McArdle (midwife) who came early. Doctor came at 12 and went again. Baby third born at 3 p.m. Doctor came at 3.30. Janie by 4.30 train. Got over it well and strong for which Thank God.'

The baby was baptized Elizabeth (although always known as Elsie) and Sarah Anne was tense and frightened by every little upset for some time, but by 12 October she noted that the baby was flourishing. Her last entry for 1887 was: 'Usual unpleasantness with Sarah and Gran. Heaven knows if I haven't the unhappy life and I see no way out of it but Providence may open up some way for us.'

1888 followed a similar pattern as previous years for Sarah Anne with the same tensions and feelings of being neglected by Robert, although she was reluctant to acknowledge them. Lizzie (his sister) frequently accompanied him to social events and, of course he had the usual fairs and cattle shows to attend, both for buying and selling stock. He attended assizes and his local vestry meetings as well as making occasional visits to church synods in

Dublin.

Robert also took part in hunts in the neighbourhood. Sarah Anne frequently mentioned that she and other members of the household had tea at the 'Castle'. This may have been Castle Howard near Avoca which was connected with the FitzWilliam Estate. Mr Edge was the agent of this part of the estate and therefore Mrs Edge and the Lawrensons, with their connections with the Shillelagh Coolattin Estate, would have been on visiting terms for afternoon tea.

Elsie was some comfort to Sarah Anne but she never ceased to grieve for her two dead children. She was again pregnant and on 15 December, 1888, with her faithful sister Janie again in attendance, her baby Winifred Jane was born.

1889 brought the added care of the new baby. In June she noted: 'Gran fell outside and got one of her attacks', and there were many references to Mrs Lawrenson's poor state of health until she died on 17 July. Two days later Sarah Anne wrote: 'The poor Grannie laid in Glenealy graveyard. A day I won't easily forget.'

1890 saw increasing responsibility and hard work for Sarah Anne and continuing rows with her difficult sister-in-law. There was yet another pregnancy, resulting in the birth of Anna Theodora (known as Dora) born on 23 July. Sarah Anne was aided by Janie, and commented again: 'Very thankful to have got on so well.'

In 1891 Sarah Anne was fully occupied running the house, helping with the domestic side of the farm and trying to manage the maids who frequently were mentioned as giving notice. Lizzie seemed a reasonable person to deal with, but was plagued with bad headaches. Sarah Anne continued to have quarrels with Sarah Lawrenson who was a great trial to them all, being a woman of great mood-swings and fits of depression. She rarely refers to Jane, the fourth sister-in-law, who seemed to cope mainly with the cooking, as Sarah Anne often mentioned fruit-picking, churning and caring for animals, but otherwise kept to her room as much as possible.

In 1892 Sarah Anne was again pregnant and Lucy Olive was born on 1 June. Janie was with her, then took Elsie and Winnie away to stay with relatives and returned again that night. Sarah Anne, at thirty-seven, was getting considerably more assertive by then as she noted on 10 June: 'I gave Robert a great feathering which I think I could hardly help. Goodness forgive me.' This word 'feathering' was a family expression meaning something stronger than a scolding—more like 'tore strips off him'! It may have derived from energetic plucking of fowl which would have been a familiar chore to all these women. By the end of June she noted: 'I cross and fighting. A miserable day.' Earlier in her marriage she would have been crying.

Sarah Anne had a holiday with the two younger children at Stratnakelly in July. This she enjoyed, seeing a good many friends. The weather seemed particularly bad during August and September of that year. For example, she noted that Robert was unable to attend Wicklow fair on 30 August as there was such a downpour, and there were many other similar days when plans had to be altered. She also referred to poor prices for stock and to finances being tight.

During November Winnie was not well and was brought to the doctor, but an unusual entry was that Robert went to the doctor on 18 November and again three days later, as he was not at all well. However, Sarah Anne noted on 27 November that Robert and Lizzie were out at church.

There is then a wide blank in her diary marked with XXXXXXXXXXXXXX until she resumed on 10 December: 'I could not write the events of the last few days. It is beyond my power. God help us all!' What she could not bring herself to write was that Robert had died of pneumonia on 1 December. Janie came yet again to assist her afflicted sister.

A possible explanation of the difficulties with Sarah Lawrenson is a story within the family that she was disfigured by smallpox and would only leave the house to walk after dark. It was said that she was missing for a long time on a wet night in November 1892 and that Robert went searching for her, and that this resulted in his swift death from pneumonia, as he had already been unwell. While not referred to directly in the diaries, this might explain some of the bitterness and rages of Sarah Lawrenson throughout her life. She lived until 1924 and was buried in her parents' grave at Glenealy graveyard.

Sarah Anne rallied and coped with the new responsibilities very quickly, but her final entry for 1892 was: 'Saturday 31 December. Last day of old year and last I suppose in Ballinakill. Lazy and depressed, though I've much to be thankful for yet. Children well and good health myself but Robert is gone and that is a blank can never be filled. The Lord help me to follow him and to bring up my children well.' Robert had died a few months after their ninth wedding anniversary. On 23 October 1888 she had written: 'Fifth anniversary of wedding day. I wonder will I live to see five more, or will they be equally unhappy!' Life did change for her before another five years had passed, but the change filled her with loneliness and imposed tremendous responsibility which she faced with great courage.

CHAPTER 4

1893–1909

Sarah Anne's first entry in her diary for 1 January 1893 was: 'My first New Year a widow. Dull, depressed and cross. Our Tom and I up fields in evening.' This was nostalgic, as during the years of her marriage to Robert going up the fields seemed to be the only little bit of daytime privacy and relaxation they had together.

In March there was a furniture auction at Ballinakill and she was very busy and depressed before it. She made arrangements to take a cottage near Wicklow. Robert had died without having made a will and Letters of Administration were granted to Sarah Anne as widow. She was paid £900 as her share of Robert's estate and also noted that the total furniture auction receipts amounted to £727/12/2. She felt that she had been fleeced by Saunders, the auctioneer.

On 15 March she and her four little girls moved to the small cottage known as 'Marlton' near Wicklow town. She must have had sufficient grazing for a cow as by 20 March she was churning with a borrowed churn and sending butter by her daily maid for sale in Wicklow. During May she sold gooseberries and commented on feeling 'dull and depressed beyond expression.' During the hot summer she worked hard and frequently was tired and 'in doleful dumps.' During August she went into town 'hardly able to walk with fatigue'.

In September 1893 she mentioned the marriage of her sister Lizzie Hopkins at Stratnakelly but, presumably because of mourning, Sarah Anne did not attend the wedding. This sister married Joseph Boyd, Assistant County Surveyor of Wicklow, and they lived at Drummin Lodge, Ballinglen, near Tinahely.

Another bit of family lore was that during these first years of widowhood, when Sarah Anne was struggling to make ends meet and caring for the four very young children, a 'foundling' was left on her doorstep. This word was used to describe a newly-born abandoned baby. Presumably some distraught pregnant woman had noted the kind maternal air of Sarah Anne and thought she would care for another child. Sarah Anne felt that she could not take on further responsibilities and with great regret she brought the child to an orphanage.

On 15 February 1894 Sarah Anne noted: 'Nana dead seven years. How hardened I have grown.' (She always referred to the daughter Ethel who died at eleven months as Nana). Anne Alford, her sisters and her brother Tom visited her frequently in the months after she left Ballinakill, but less so as time went on, and in June 1894 she wrote: 'Feeling dull and forsaken. Oh poor Robert, how I miss him.' There were numerous references to the extremes of weather, especially awful snow in February 1895 and, of course, there were many the ailments of the four children which made her very tense and anxious.

In April 1897 Sarah Anne moved to Dublin, purchasing a house in Moyne Road, Ranelagh where she planned to take lodgers to augment her small dividends. This move was probably encouraged by some of Robert's nephews who were helpful to her. Samuel Lawrenson advanced a loan for the purchase of the house and Ernest Lawrenson, a stockbroker, helped her with financial advice for a number of years. John Hopkins and his sister Anna, first cousins of Sarah Anne, lived in Belgrave Square, Rathmines and provided friendship and stability during her time in Dublin.

Sarah Anne had a very busy few months buying furniture at auctions, getting the house organised and entering the four children in the Protestant National School in Rathgar Avenue. By August she had two lodgers and in September, when the girls went to school, she was a bit freer, though when the weather was very wet she kept them at home. She went to church regularly, brought the girls to Sunday school and enjoyed musical events in

St Matthias's Church in Hatch Street.

Having lived in a small terrace house at 38 South Circular Road for a time, in August 1901 Sarah Anne moved to 155 Rathmines Road, taking some lodgers with her. This was a much larger, four-storeyed house near Portobello Bridge. She must have asked Mrs Scott, who had been with her for nearly two years, to give a reference for the reletting of a flat, and the following was given:

> 155 Rathmines Rd.,
> Rathmines,
> Dublin

> Mrs Scott has great pleasure in recommending a flat at the above address which she is only giving up on being obliged to leave Ireland. The rooms are large and bright, the sitting-room having a pantry off, and the large bedroom a bath-room with hot and cold water laid on. Punctuality, good cooking, and perfect cleanliness, combined with a cheerful readiness to oblige in every way, have made a home from which both Mr and Mrs Scott greatly regret to part. They have been with Mrs Lawrenson for nearly two years, and feel they cannot speak too highly of her continual consideration and kind attention. The neighbourhood of Rathmines is well-known as one of the prettiest suburbs of Dublin, and is convenient for the city, the house being only a few yards from Portobello Bridge (ld tram fare). Mrs Lawrenson would show the rooms at any time desired by advertiser.
> 3 October 1902

Sarah Anne kept up a friendly correspondence with Mrs Scott for some years.

She must have become an excellent manager to combine long term lettings and overnight casuals (frequently relations) with only one daily help, named

Ellen Gorman, who helped with the laundry, which must have been considerable. Ellen was a most reliable stand-by for as long as Sarah Anne needed domestic help and was regarded with great affection by the family.

The constant supplying of simple but adequate meals for such varying numbers must have been difficult, especially on such a limited budget. Understandably, Sarah Anne's diary for the early years of the 1900s was largely devoted to accounts, with very brief comments as to visits from Wicklow relatives.

For the first week of June 1902 she received the following rents:

2 June	
Mr and Mrs Crawford	9/0
Miss Hawker	4/0
Misses Chambers	6/0
Mr and Mrs Scott	12/0
Mr Vickery	7/6
	£1/18/6

Payments during the same week were listed:

2 June	
Goods	1/9
ditto	11d
Ellen	4/6
8 June	
Milk	2/3
Rates	£6/6/9
	£6/9/0
	6d.
	7d.
	3/4
	2/10
	7/3
Saturday's shopping	£1/4./1
	£8/7/0

She was receiving a rent of £11 per quarter for the house in Moyne Road and had some dividends, so these helped to balance her books.

In March 1902 she noted a rent from a William Kingston of Skibbereen, who was sitting a law examination at this time, while apprenticed to his cousin Jasper Wolfe. Sarah Anne's rent book also showed receipts from Mrs and the Misses Kingston for short periods when they came to Dublin to attend the Annual Methodist Conference. The Kingston sisters ran a school in Skibbereen and were lively talkative people who became friendly with Sarah Anne. In due course this led to their brother, Samuel Kingston, renting a room from her in January 1903 when he took up employment in the civil service. He continued as a paying guest/lodger until June 1911, moving wherever the family went, and becoming a good friend to the whole family before becoming Lucy's suitor in 1912.

Also in January 1903, Sarah Anne received a letter from her sister Janie announcing her engagement and she felt sore about it, as she had not known of its likelihood. Janie later married Thomas Jones and went to live at Ballinglen House, Tinahely, directly opposite Drummin Lodge where her sister Lizzie was raising a large family. She had her eighth baby in 1905. Their brother Tom married Anna Woodburne in February 1903. In 1894 he had moved from Stratnakelly to a house nearer Shillelagh. It was known as Cronalea and had a millwheel attached. This house and the other family homes were holiday venues for Sarah Anne's daughters over the years, their aunts frequently having them to stay for short periods two at a time. Lizzie Lawrenson married William FitzHenry and lived at Ballydonrea, Kilcoole and this was another house frequently visited during the girls' holidays. Sarah Anne could rarely get away from Dublin while she had her lodgers.

Elsie and Winnie both left school at the age of fourteen and started secretarial training. However, Dora was noted by her mother as showing an artistic bent, so when her schooling came to an end in 1904 it was arranged that she would be apprenticed to the McConnell Studios. The following is her apprenticeship deed:

In consideration of receiving a fee of twenty five pounds, I agree to Anna Theodora Lawrenson becoming my pupil for a term of four years—and I further agree to teach her and cause her to be taught and instructed in the arts of Illuminating and Heraldry and to supply her with all necessary materials to accomplish those Arts and during the first year I shall pay her the sum of £5/4/0., during the second year £10/0/0., during the third year £13/0/0 and during the fourth year the sum of £19/10/0 in consideration of her giving me her services daily (Sundays excepted) between the hours of 9.30 o'clock a.m. and 6 o'clock p.m. with one and a half hours interval for five days of the week, no interval to occur on Saturdays when her services shall cease at 2 o'clock p.m. Anna Theodora Lawrenson undertaking not to enter into any other employment or to give her services to any other person without permission and to faithfully serve in all matters appertaining to the work during the hours and term specified.
James McConnell

I agree to become the pupil of James McConnell under the above terms—on the condition that during the first year I work half time for the first six months and three-quarter time during the second six months. (sixpenny postage stamp)
This 9th day of May 1904
Anna Theodora Lawrenson

Witness: Sarah Anne Lawrenson.

The terms of this deed seem rigorous for a fourteen year old, and one feels relief at seeing the hours modified for the first year. It seemed to set the tone for Dora as she was a most hardworking and dedicated artist almost all her life.

James McConnell (1842–1916) had established a heraldic studio in Lincoln Place and was regarded as one of the most celebrated masters of the art in Europe. He had three daughters all of whom trained with him. One of them, Mabel, took up a position in the Office of Arms in Dublin Castle. Mabel and Ruby continued to run the studio after their father's death in 1916. The work included illuminated addresses to various dignatories (some of them royal), tributes to people who were retiring or clergy moving parishes and even an elaborate menu for a banquet in celebration of Her Majesty's jubilee given in The Royal College of Surgeons Ireland by Sir William Stokes, President, on 23 April 1887. This was probably designed as well as executed by James McConnell.

Part of Dora's training involved researching and executing heraldic coats of arms. The studio also provided careful training in Celtic art. At the founding of the Free State, Mabel and Ruby McConnell supplied the originals for postage and fiscal stamps which were of elaborate celtic design, and a very plain practical bilingual Customs Stamp.

From 1906 all four girls were earning: Elsie in the Telephone Department of the Post Office, Winnie as a legal secretary, Dora as an apprentice illuminator and Lucy in a secretarial position in Greenmount Oil Company. Sarah Anne was therefore able to move to a smaller terrace house in Lower Beechwood Avenue, Ranelagh, and take fewer lodgers, thus easing her work load, but retaining the congenial company of Samuel Kingston. She arranged for Elsie to begin singing lessons with Miss Frances McConnell, but commented: 'Troubles begin again with Winnie's boys', i.e. male admirers. These references to Winnie's boys become more and more frequent, as do references to the consequent rows about late nights. The two sisters, so near in age, were different in character. Elsie was a very serene and steady character and from very early a confidante of her mother. Winnie was extremely moody and rebelled against Sarah Anne's attempts at strict discipline. She was attractive, with a neat waist and piled-up curly fair hair and she enjoyed flirting. However, she and Elsie later took a very serious interest in the women's suffrage movement.

Winnie also became involved with the Dickens Fellowship, which was a popular association of Dickens enthusiasts. The fellowship arranged readings of his works, ran socials, dances and whist drives, and also organised dinners for the poor each Christmas and New Year. These annual dinners for the poor were the only indication that the Lawrensons were aware of the great poverty in Dublin during these years. They all worked long and hard to support themselves, so they had not much margin for social work, but Winnie did expend much of her energy on this fellowship and all aspects of its work and shared her enthusiasm with the family.

As Sarah Anne's domestic duties got lighter, she paid visits to relations and friends, to those among her acquaintance who were sick or had new babies. She generally revealed herself as a person very much able to enter into the cares and joys of others, doubtless because of her own experiences. She was anxious to give her daughters every chance of a wider education in keeping with their tastes and abilities and by means of careful budgeting of their always limited resources.

CHAPTER 5
1910–1915

Sarah Anne's relations from Wicklow often dropped in to see her, often unexpectedly. Sometimes they paid overnight visits but at other times just visited briefly, when attending cattle markets, keeping dental appointments or just shopping. The rail service was also much used for parcels, as the various farming relations frequently sent gifts of poultry, eggs and sacks of potatoes.

Sarah Anne also had increasing contact with Robert's family as Thomas Dowse Lawrenson (Robert's brother) retired from his position as under-agent to Earl FitzWilliam at Coolattin Estate (a position similar to that of his elder brother Ralph). He and his wife, always referred to as 'Sarah Tom' to distinguish her from all the other Sarahs in the family, moved from Ballykelly to a house in Dartmouth Square, Ranelagh. They were both good friends of Sarah Anne and she regularly visited there. Her daughters were fond of their cousins and were 'greatly fretted' when the Lawrensons' son, another Ralph, died of typhoid in 1907, aged seventeen .

A studio photograph of the Lawrenson family group was taken in 1910 and it is interesting to compare it with the one taken when they first arrived in Dublin in 1897. Lucy's expression is very determined in both photographs.

The first mention of Women's Suffrage Association meetings by Sarah Anne is her noting that Elsie attended one in Dublin in May 1910 and another in Kingstown in June. Mrs Millicent Fawcett, a well-known British suffrage speaker, had addressed a suffrage meeting in Dublin with much publicity and this may have interested Elsie and Winnie. Winnie was soon selling 'Votes for Women' badges at Unionist meetings and also distributing suffrage leaflets. She was increasingly independent and there were repeated references to 'unpleasantness with Winnie' as a result. All four girls cycled round Dublin and so did Sarah Anne, but by 1911 she had graduated to a sturdy tricycle. She noted in May 1911: 'I am fifty-six years old and strong and well, thank God'.

The steady contributions from all girls into the family exchequer enabled Sarah Anne to stop taking paying guests and to move to a smaller house. Therefore Samuel Kingston (or Sambo, as he was then affectionately called by the family) reluctantly parted from them. The Lawrensons moved to the north side of Dublin, taking a house in Lindsay Road, Glasnevin in June 1911.

Elsie was a clerical assistant to Gilbert Sutcliffe, a telephone engineer in the post office. His work necessitated frequent visits to England and it became customary for Elsie to keep his wife company during his absence and help with the care of their young family. Through this there developed a long-standing and warm friendship between the two families but, with a formality typical of those times, Sarah Anne always referred to her as 'Mrs Sutcliffe' rather than using her Christian name.

In July 1911 Winnie entered for a National Education Examination, obtained second place and for the next fifteen years worked in the Education Office in Marlborough Street. She was still very much involved with the Dickens Fellowship and sometimes contributed papers which were read out at meetings. Sarah Anne attended one of these meetings and was proud of her daughter's achievement. This did not prevent continuing adverse comments about Winnie such as: 'Winnie to Dickens dance alone. Not home till 3.20. Usual ructions.' Winnie also kept up her interest in the suffrage movement, serving on the committee of the Women's Suffrage Association in 1911 and acting as steward at a meeting for Christabel Pankhurst.

As a result of moving to the north side of the city, Sarah

Anne heard of the musical Harrison family and arranged to have both Lucy and Dora's voices trained by Robert Harrison. Elsie became a paid singer in Tullow Church, Carrickmines and Lucy took on a similar position in Baggotrath Church in Baggot Street. The custom was to employ one or two singers with trained voices who then attended each service and led the amateur choirs in the hymns, psalms and anthems sung during the services. This entailed regular church attendance but sometimes the girls could substitute for one another.

Sarah Anne enjoyed musical concerts and noted the names of performers Madame Nora Borel and William Watts around this time. They were still popular soloists during the 1930s and 1940s, so they had very long careers.

In October 1912 Sarah Anne paid a two-day visit to her sister-in-law Lizzie FitzHenry at Ballydonrea near Kilcoole and Anne and Robert Alford visited her there. It seems clear that quite cordial feelings existed once the women did not have to live together.

Christmas Day 1912 was described by Sarah Anne: 'Fine morning but came very heavy showers. Elsie to Carrickmines (service) home straight to dinner. Winnie and I to 10 o'clock Communion Service in St Aidan's. Winnie to Dickens dinner (for poor). Dora to St George's Church. Lucy to Baggotrath and sang solo in carols. A pleasant quiet evening all together. Lots of post.'

She continued reporting that on St Stephen's Day Elsie 'went for short time to office' and that Lucy and Dora were at work as usual. Work was hard and hours were long in those days and the number of public holidays very limited. This was especially true for Lucy in the telegraph office, but this was accepted as normal.

1913 was to prove a very eventful year for the family and a great test of Sarah Anne's wisdom and patience. It started badly: '1 January. A fearful row at night and Winnie dashed out. Very weary of it all and don't know how it will end.'

On 21 June, Sam Kingston proposed to Lucy who promptly refused him. Sarah Anne was very concerned about this as she had a great regard for Swik (which was Lucy's name for him from now on) and must have been aware of his intentions. She wrote to him in June and again in August ('Hope I'm doing right.') as she had observed how upset Lucy was during these months. Swik came and had a long talk with her ('Girls not to know but I told Elsie.'). The outcome was a happy one for all but is dealt with more fully in Lucy's life.

Concurrent with this upheaval was a more unexpected one involving Dora's sudden engagement to George Bell. Dora appeared to have had a very docile adolescence in comparison to her sister Winnie, but her early twenties were not so calm as regards the opposite sex. In July 1913 Dora set off for Kilkee for a holiday with her sister Elsie. Sarah Anne was annoyed to receive a letter on 2 August saying they were staying a few days longer. The two girls arrived back from Killarney on 4 August and there followed 'great and exciting talk, chiefly about Mr Bell.'

The following day Dora and her mother dined together and Dora wrote her first letter to Mr George Bell. Her mother was feeling very excited and upset, as Sarah Anne confided to Janie by letter. Dora had fallen in love with George Bell and had become engaged during the holiday. He was a mercurial person living on a family estate in Leitrim. He came to visit on 28 August and then consulted Sarah Anne, but she felt 'tired and tormented', as it had all happened too quickly for her to assimilate. By 5 September there was a great upset between mother and daughter that left Dora in tears.

On 17 September Dora went to visit George Bell at his family home and ten days later wrote a most depressed letter to her mother, but later seemed to come to terms with 'Brother Bell', as he was known in her family. She returned from Leitrim on 3 October and had a serious talk with her mother. Next day Dora spent engrossing a deed and writing a long letter to Leitrim. On 5 October Dora spent some time in bed 'in doleful dumps' (the expressive family description) but rose about 4 o'clock and had a great 'confab' with Swik, and this may have helped to clear her mind. On 30 December Dora received a letter from George Bell referring to the possibility of his going abroad, which upset her. When Dora had another long and unpleasant letter from George Bell on 2 January 1914, she wrote offering him his liberty. A fortnight later she received a lettercard from him confirming that their relationship was all over, but by January 27 she had a long apologetic letter, and recommenced correspondence with him. He proposed again on 14 February (St Valentine's Day!).

There followed an uneasy and detached engagement, with occasional visits being exchanged. On 22 August Dora received a long and sad letter from him and a further exchange of lettercards followed, but both must have realised that it was all over. All this excitement over Lucy and Dora must have aroused Winnie's jealousy; as Sarah Anne noted: 'Swik here and Winnie unpleasant'. As Swik was already such an intimate friend of Sarah Anne, having been like a son to her during the eight years of sharing their home, she found great comfort in being able to consult him about Dora's uneasy relationship with George Bell. She also spent nearly a week in Co. Wicklow visiting and telling Janie about the affair.

Sarah Anne's increased leisure enabled her to broaden her sources of entertainment. We have seen in the past how musical events in churches seemed all she would consider. Now, with the encouragement of her daughters, she attended the Abbey Theatre, musical events such as Gilbert and Sullivan performances at the Gaiety Theatre and also became quite keen on the cinema (then, of course, silent films). The girls sometimes organised these outings for their mother as, witness, for instance, Sarah Anne's entry in March 1914: 'D'Oyley Carte Company doing

Gilbert and Sullivan at Gaiety. Go with Elsie to *Mikado*. Dora's treat. Lovely.' In July Sarah Anne went with Elsie for a short holiday to Wales.

On 2 August, 1914 Sarah Anne noted: 'A Sunday *Times* on account of War'—presumably there was not normally a Sunday printing. Then on 4 August: 'War declared between England and Germany. Great excitement and prices of everything up.' A few days later Sarah Anne went to St Patrick's Cathedral to a service in which there were prayers for the war. By 16 August she noted: 'Troops and horses going all day. Things very sad and depressed.' In September she commented that Elsie had gone to an ambulance lecture in preparation for being able to render aid to wounded returning soldiers.

Sarah Anne's entry for 27 October was: 'Lucy's wedding day. We all up very early and to St George's in taxi. Home and all over before 9 o'clock—a long, lonely day. Card from Lucy *Kingston* from Warrenpoint in the evening.' Postal services were certainly efficient at that period! Two days later Sarah Anne received a long letter from Lucy and by 31 October the newly-weds had returned. Sarah Anne obviously found it hard to adjust to the thought of Lucy, her youngest, now living independently though very near her. Her entry for 2 November was: 'I over with parcels to Lucy. First time to see her in her own home and it was not pleasant. Lucy called on her way down town and to market—swelled head.'

Sarah Anne had plenty of other preoccupations to help her over this period of adjustment as Dora, having managed to extricate herself from the George Bell situation, had had a proposal from a much more suitable young man, William Harrison, but refused him.

The entire Harrison family was well known to the Lawrensons. Richard Harrison, the father of five sons, was an engineer but also an organist. He played a church organ in Booterstown for twenty-one years and for thirty-seven years in the Free Church in Dublin. He combined this activity with running an engineering firm in Sackville Place, employing four of his sons. His son George became a full-time organist and teacher, having studied at the Royal Irish Academy under Sir Robert Prescott Stewart, and had the distinction of playing the organ in the same parish for seventy-five years, seventy of them in St George's Church. Robert had a fine voice and taught singing, and Thomas was a pianist.

William was the youngest son and his mother had died when he was barely two years old. He and his brothers were brought up by their aunt Mary Bond Harrison to whom he was deeply attached. He began his musical education in the Royal Irish Academy of Music, also under Sir Robert Prescott Stewart. He then studied with August Wilhelmj in London and with his son Adolph in Dublin. He gave violin recitals in the Antient Concert Rooms in Dublin, accompanied by his brother George, in 1905 and 1906, once in a 'command' performance for a visit of the British Princess Royal.

He was first mentioned in Sarah Anne's and Lucy's diaries as 'Angel Face' or 'Seraph' because of his serene expression. It was a few years before Lucy's slightly mocking name of 'Liam' finally became common among the Lawrensons. His own family always called him Willie and probably disapproved of the Liam appellation, being strongly West British in their outlook, as was Liam himself.

Liam must have been aware of the end of Dora's second engagement to George Bell. By 27 September, 1914 he had proposed but was immediately refused, greatly to Sarah Anne's regret. She wrote several private letters to Liam, encouraging his suit. She had a 'great talk' with Dora, and Liam's gentle perseverance began to have results, as Dora regularly allowed him to escort her home from choir practice. By Christmas Eve he had presented Dora with a gold watch, but she was noted by Sarah Anne to be very dull and down in spirits. She continued to be so depressed that her mother was very puzzled about her.

During 1915 Sarah Anne was very preoccupied with Dora's affairs but made occasional comments about the war and noted that on 7 May: 'Lusitania torpedoed—a terrible disaster.' Next day was her sixtieth birthday 'Thank God for health and many blessings.'

In July, 'Dora and I took a wild notion and went to Bohemia Pictures' and in December, 'Elsie and I to *Iolanthe* by the Rathmines Amateur Company in Gaiety'— presumably the precursor of the Rathmines and Rathgar Musical Society of later years.

CHAPTER SIX
1916–1928

1916 was an eventful year in many ways. On 6 April, Sarah Anne went to Ballydonrea as William FitzHenry had died. 'A long and weary day I am not likely to forget.' This was the realisation that Lizzie was failing mentally and would need care; Sarah Anne agreed to take her to live as a paying guest in Lindsay Road. By 19 April she was installed, but was too confused to be left alone so the girls took turns in helping their mother and bringing their aunt for walks.

By 24 April: 'Dreadful accounts of Sinn Féin Rebellion. Gas cut off. No one to business. GPO taken over. Neither post nor paper. A terrible time.' On 27 April, Sarah Anne continued: 'Fourth day of this dreadful excitement. Electric light taken. Great fires down town. Things awful.' Next day, 'Lovely day, but bad news from the fires. Great work to get anything from the shops.' Lucy's diary dealt more fully with these events, as will be seen in Part II of this book.

In September Winnie took her mother to the Abbey Theatre to see *John Bull's Other Island* and Sarah Anne enjoyed the break. However, by the middle of November the Dartmouth Square Lawrensons must have agreed to take Lizzie FitzHenry and Sarah (Tom) collected her. Sarah Anne commented in her diary 'Very glad to be alone', but by 29 November poor Lizzie had returned, and Sarah Anne and the girls resumed responsibility for her.

Sarah Anne's entry for 18 February 1917 was: 'Edith Lawrenson died. Gave us a great shock. Buried in Shillelagh.' This was the elder daughter of Thomas and Sarah Lawrenson of Dartmouth Square, but the cause of her death was not specified. Edith had been poorly throughout January and this might explain why so much of the care of Lizzie Lawrenson was left to Sarah Anne. As St Patrick's Day approached, there must have been rumours that there might be another rebellion, as Sarah Anne noted on 17 March: 'Feared rising but thank God for a quiet ending to the day.'

By 17 April it was arranged that Lizzie FitzHenry would go into a nursing home. That evening Sarah Anne's entry was: 'All to hear *Creation* at St George's. It seems strange to be without the care of P.G.' and two days later 'We feel a great freedom.' No wonder, as they had taken full charge of a very confused and delicate old woman for an entire year.

Liam Harrison was an unusually talented man with a great capacity for hard work, but he seemed to be dogged by financial worries and bad luck for much of his life. He was a qualified engineer, a fine violin and viola performer, and an expert cabinet maker and craftsman, but nevertheless found it very difficult to earn a living. Consequently, he and Dora had a prolonged engagement, but by September 1917 they were househunting. With financial help from Winnie, the family bought 'Mirtna', 19 Iona Drive, Glasnevin, selling 73 Lindsay Road for £515. On 29 October, Sarah Anne with Elsie, Winnie and Dora moved to the new house and two days later Liam left to take a position in Ross Engineering firm in Stockport in England. Dora was relieved to receive a wire before 2 o'clock the same day to say that he had crossed the dangerously mined Irish Sea safely. There was a great blizzard of snow and a hurricane of wind on 16 December but Liam arrived back safely at the end of December.

Dora married Liam on 4 January 1918 and they caught the mailboat *Leinster* (later torpedoed) and proceeded to Stockport immediately, as Liam had only very brief leave. They returned together in February and, as things seemed to be very uneasy with Liam's employment, Dora remained at Mirtna when he went back. The rest of 1918 followed much the same pattern with she sometimes in Stockport, but by the end of the year Dora had settled permanently at Mirtna and went back to work at the McConnell Studio. Liam came back for good in January

1919 so the Stockport interlude ended.

One by one the family contracted the dreaded Spanish influenza and all were desolated at Elsie's death from it. This is dealt with more fully in Lucy's life. Dora was a great support to her mother over this tragic period, accompanying her on visits to Elsie's grave and running the household, and Ralph, Sarah Anne's beloved grandson, kept them from 'moping', as they helped Lucy constantly by taking charge of him.

In September Dora told her mother she was pregnant. This cheered Sarah Anne, but in November all were saddened by the death of Thomas Dowse Lawrenson of Dartmouth Square. The following February Lizzie Fitz-Henry died and in due course Sarah Anne and the three girls received legacies for which they were very thankful.

On 11 May 1920 Dora had a daughter, Elizabeth Mary, and Sarah Anne's diary note was 'Dora splendid and a fine Elizabeth.' They were back at 'Mirtna' by May 26 and in June Dora was again working at deeds and illuminating addresses, with Sarah Anne happily caring for Elizabeth. As well as executing her more formal orders, Dora frequently presented various family members with their favourite poem or quotation beautifully illuminated and framed. These were much prized gifts and the colours glow to the present day.

The period known as 'The Troubles' in 1921 created great difficulties for all citizens. On his way to St George's Church Liam found himself in a serious ambush, from which he had a miraculous escape.

Towards the end of the year there was a possibility that Winnie would be asked to move to Belfast by the civil service. The suggestion that they might all go did not appeal to Sarah Anne. Early in 1922 Winnie was still undecided, but she finally gave up the idea, and then came the first mention of Frederick Budds, whom she met at a walking group called the Ramblers' Club.

The family were becoming inured to ambushes: Winnie and Lucy narrowly escaped one when attending the

Abbey Theatre in September; Janie and Dora just missed one near Harcourt Street Station in December and in January 1923 Winnie and Dora had great difficulty getting home from St George's because of a great ambush. When lecturing in the USA in the 1930s, Dora reminisced on being lined up on two occasions with her family 'with a view to, possibly, being shot by the Black and Tans, later by the Irish Republican Army—the left wing of the Sinn Féiners' This period is dealt with more fully in Part II.

Winnie generously provided a motor car for Liam and he took them all out for drives which were a great novelty. Liam was taking pupils for evening violin lessons and Dora was pursuing her various art assignments, but money was very scarce. Dora therefore answered advertisements regarding paying guests and in October Donn Piatt joined the household in this capacity. He was the grandson of Dr Sigerson, author and Celtic scholar, and a nephew of Dora Sigerson Shorter, the poet. He was a young student of Celtic languages at this period and suffered greatly from asthma, so his mother Hester Piatt frequently visited to help with his attacks. Donn Piatt became a good friend of the family in Glasnevin and, when the Kingstons moved to Dalkey, continued to visit them there.

On 4 June Liam and Dora took Elizabeth to school for the first time. Later she was very rebellious and in September Dora had to resort to force to get her to school again. She may have been reacting to the atmosphere of strain in the household, as Winnie and Budds were having frequent disagreements and poor Liam was said to be at his lowest ebb, as he had decided that he must emigrate and consulted the American consul. He obtained a passport by the middle of March, 1925. There was much business to be attended to in the sale of 'Mirtna' and the leasing of a flat at Vesey Place, Monkstown during April. Here Sarah Anne, Winnie, Dora and Elizabeth were to live in his absence.

On 11 May 1925 (Elizabeth's fifth birthday) Liam sailed from North Wall. Sarah Anne was almost as distressed as

Dora at the parting, as she had become increasingly fond of him over the years and he was said to revere his mother-in-law. She wrote 'God knows how or when we will see him again'—and, alas, she never did.

Dora was now a 'grass widow' and the next three years were worrying for her as the news from Liam kept fluctuating. He reached Seattle by 18 June and wired to report safe arrival, having travelled by sea via the Panama Canal. He wrote a cheerful and encouraging letter to Sarah Anne, though he had not anything definite to report. The next letter to Dora was 'doleful' and left her very depressed. However, by September he was able to send some money and in December reported that he had a position as first violin in a big orchestra at £600 per annum. This was a great relief to the whole family, but the appointment proved to be only short term.

Elizabeth developed whooping cough in February 1926 and once again Sarah Anne was a great support to Dora in nursing her. Her grandmother sometimes took Elizabeth down to Ballinglen for holidays and there was a close relationship between the two.

Dora and Sarah Anne were very close companions too, and were united in their dismay over the fraught relationship between Winnie and Fred Budds. Despite this, the couple were househunting in Dalkey and decided to buy a small two-storeyed house called 'Riva' fronting Coliemore Road not far from Coliemore Harbour. It had a very small sloping garden at the rear and then a dramatic seascape with large granite boulders bounding Dalkey Sound, a channel between the mainland and Dalkey Island, with swift tidal currents which could be dangerous for bathing.

It was planned that Sarah Anne, Dora and Elizabeth would live with them, but endless serious rows kept recurring between Winnie and Fred, so plans were very hard to establish. Sarah Anne was not happy about this proposed marriage, as Fred was a very quiet self-contained man and Winnie was an outgoing, generous and sociable person. The constant quarrels seemed a warning against such a match but the stubborn Winnie would not be influenced. Eventually Sarah Anne and Dora gave up their flat and moved into 'Riva' on April 23. Winnie left her office and was presented with a clock.

On a lovely morning on 6 May 1926 Winnie and Fred were married in Dalkey at 8 o'clock and left for Portrush. Dora and Sarah Anne went for a walk up Vico Road after tea that evening and revelled in the scenery. On that same day Liam wrote a long affectionate letter to Sarah Anne which included the following:

I was delighted to get your kind letter and know that you are all right again. I could not tell you how upset I was to hear that you were ill. I know only too well that in every way this has been a very trying time on you and that you will be thankful to get settled in the new home, and I have sure confidence that you will find in Fred Budds a kind and affectionate son-in-law. With regard to your kind remarks about me, I may say it has always been a very great 'fret' to me that it has not been in my power to do more to put comfort and happiness into your life in return for the love and kindness you have ever bestowed on me. I know well you wish me back and I wish it a thousand times more myself. If there was the smallest prospect for me it would not take me two minutes to decide, for the loneliness here is not a thing that I could ever describe. You are all very very much in my thoughts to-day wondering how Winnie's wedding went off and what it was all like.

Dora had to struggle against depression, especially as she noticed her mother failing a little and tiring much more easily. She felt she should stay in Ireland, though aware of Liam's loneliness. Liam, faced with the uncertainties of his life in the States, felt he had to unload some of his worries but, when the news was really depressing, he wrote privately to Lucy and Swik, asking them to shield Dora if they thought necessary.

In June 1927 Dora and Elizabeth went for a six-month visit to Seattle. They returned in November, having a better picture of what life in USA would be like. By the beginning of 1928 Dora began to make enquiries about emigration. To meet the requirements of the US Immigration Authorities, she applied to her cousin for a reference and he sent her the following:

> St Luke's Rectory, South Circular Road, Dublin.
> 3 April 1928
>
> A. Mrs Anna Theodora Harrison née Lawrenson is well known to me from her childhood about thirty years.
> B. She has never been in a prison nor an almshouse.
> C. She has never served in nor had connection with armed forces.
> D. She did not serve in an industrial plant during the Great War.
> E. She is most honest, sober, industrious and capable. I know her intimately. She is my cousin in the second degree.
>
> Thomas Haskins Seale, Rector of St Nicholas and St Luke's Parish. Ex. Sch. Mod. M.A. T.C.D.

Both Dora and Winnie must have noticed Sarah Anne's increasing weariness but could not persuade her to cut down on her activities. Elizabeth was actually sharing her bed when she realised her grandmother was ill during the early hours of 29 April 1928 and raised the alarm. The local doctor was called but Sarah Anne's brave heart had stopped before he or Lucy and Swik had arrived.

PART II

Lucy Olive Kingston

CHAPTER SEVEN
1892 –1912

When Sarah Anne was first widowed, she prayed for strength to bring up her children well. Her faith sustained her and she developed wisdom in drawing out the potential of each daughter. We have seen the steadfast, idealistic Elsie, the fiercely independent but generous and sociable Winnie and the quiet, witty, artistic Dora living and working together as a team.

The second part of this book is a more detailed study of Lucy, the youngest, who took her place in this family team but who had a more questioning and adventurous mind than her sisters and whose contacts and cultural interests were much wider than her upbringing and education would have led one to expect.

Lucy was born on 1 June 1892 and her first six months were spent at Ballinakill. Sarah Anne was very busy and preoccupied during that summer of financial hardship and bad weather and concerned about the ill-health of both her daughter Winnie and her husband Robert. Half jokingly, in later life, Lucy used to say that she had learned to be self-sufficient from very tender years. Though a person of strong emotions, she was remarkably undemonstrative in expressing those feelings. Swik used to comment that the Lawrensons were like a family of boys.

Being only six months old when Robert died, she never knew her father, and the various moves during the next few years would not have affected her very much. She had the continuing company of her sisters, who were all so near in age. Her closest companion would have been Dora, two years older. Winnie tended to tease her, but Lucy always deeply admired Elsie, five years her senior, and very like her in appearance, both girls resembling their father, while both Winnie and Dora were more like their mother. Dora, in particular, inherited Sarah's large expressive eyes.

The greatest event in Lucy's childhood must have been the move to Dublin and entering Rathgar Girls National School in Rathgar Avenue. She enjoyed school, often praising the subject 'Latin roots', which she felt gave an understanding of English to those to whom a more classical education was not available. On leaving school at fourteen, Lucy was presented with a handsome copy of *Self Help* by Samuel Smiles. It was inscribed to

Lucy Lawrenson for Superior Answering,
April 1906.
L. E. Johnston, Principal.

This book (written in 1859 with an updated edition in 1866 and a new edition in 1905) is subtitled as giving illustrations of conduct and perseverance. Not one example is feminine, apart from an incidental reference to the wife of an artist who helped him to save in order to study in Rome! However, this did not impair Lucy's later commitment to feminism.

Shortly after Lucy left school in 1906, the family moved to Lower Beechwood Avenue, Ranelagh. She entered Skerries Commercial College and also began a correspondence class. Her reading sounded somewhat pious, with such titles as *Stepping Heavenward* and *A Noble Life*, but by 1908 it was more romantic, as she listed *The Scarlet Pimpernel* by Baroness Orczy and Wilkie Collins's *The Moonstone* and *The Woman in White*. She owned and rode a bicycle by then and had learned to play whist. She had piano lessons and all the girls attended gymnastic classes, Elsie being particularly keen and encouraging of her sisters to persevere.

In March 1908 Lucy was given a notice about an entrance examination to the General Post Office Telegraph Department. She seemed undecided about applying, but was strongly encouraged to do so by a friend of her mother, Miss Florence Bermingham, who was employed there as supervisor. Lucy sat the test but did not succeed in getting a place, as competition for these permanent, pensionable places was keen.

On 31 March 1908 Dora and Lucy were confirmed at St Matthias's Church of Ireland in Hatch Street (since demolished). The four girls were regular in church attendance and Winnie was a Sunday school teacher for many years.

On 1 May Lucy got a prize for orthography (free composition) and entered a few more competitions, displaying her interest in writing at an early age—she was now approaching her sixteenth birthday.

In 1908, too, she and Elsie went to stay with Lizzie Lawrenson (then married to William FitzHenry) in Ballydonrea and enjoyed their time there. She also noted that Winnie and Dora had been at Ballykelly and returned 'bursting with news'. It was thus that the girls kept in touch with their Lawrenson aunts and cousins.

Lucy then mislaid her diary and her next entry is in January 1909 when she wrote 'Found this in hat box and deplore my neglect of it.' She noted she was sitting another Post Office examination although there were only two vacancies. As the results were not known for some months, she read Dickens's *Little Dorrit* and Charles Reade's *The Cloister and the Hearth* to steady her nerves. By 28 April she heard that she had achieved first place in the examination and was soon called to be weighed and measured and to have a medical examination. She also had to be vaccinated.

Lucy kept up her music, playing Schubert at this stage, and read *Romeo and Juliet,* having just finished *Hamlet.* She also noted: 'Reading *Jane Eyre* on my seventeenth birthday.'

On 21 June 1909: 'Begin at GPO. Conflicting opinions, on the whole good. Miss Bermingham befriends me', and next day: 'Like office better.' She learnt the Morse code and on 2 July: 'Get on to twelve words on telegraph. Like office alright. Practise economy with dinners.' She had not sufficient time to return home for a meal and was trying to stretch a very modest salary by 'tightening her belt'.

By September she was learning French and enjoyed visits to a skating rink and on 21 October she suddenly confided to her diary 'I am a suffragette.' The women's suffrage debate was by then—and remained so for the next few years—a very live issue within such societies as the Dickens Fellowship and the Young Men's Christian Association in Dublin, as well as in ordinary conversation. It became obvious that Lucy, brought up in such a female household, enjoyed the mixture of sexes and ages in her office life. Earlier in her diary she had referred almost in code to various mild flirtations and arguments (always referring to one escort as 'the enemy') but her office milieu provided more serious debate, for example: 'Mr K. argues women's brains v. men's.'

In December she bought the weekly *Irish Times* to send to her uncle Joe in Australia. She also noted: 'I am at newswire for first time for quarter of an hour.' and: 'Most severe frost and snow since 1893.' On 24 December: 'Elsie, Dora and I at carols at St Patrick's. Fearfully crushed.' This has a familiar ring to the present-day devotee!

Towards the end of January 1910: 'Awful snow. Every place stopped. Elsie and Winnie don't come home for dinner.' On 5 February: 'Great puff in paper about Mrs Fawcett's address on suffrage.' Mrs Millicent Garrett Fawcett was President of the British Union of Women Suffrage Societies and had been Vice-President of the International Alliance of Women since 1904. There were frequent visits from British suffrage speakers at this time and Winnie acted as steward at many of the meetings.

There is no indication that Dora took much part in the suffrage activities of her sisters from 1910 onwards, but she had by then become a pupil at the Dublin Municipal

School of Art 'under the fearsome teaching of Orpen (later Sir William)' as she put it herself in later life. She had as fellow students Harry Clarke and Grace Gifford, later stained glass artist and caricaturist respectively. Grace Gifford later married 1916 leader Joseph Mary Plunkett the day he was executed.

By the end of February Lucy was quite ill with high fever and suspected of having typhoid, so she got sick leave from the office and a nurse came to the house on doctor's orders to assist Sarah Anne. Lucy made good use of her time off, however, as she read Mrs Gaskell's *Wives and Daughters* and John Bunyan's *The Pilgrim's Progress*. In April she read George Eliot's *Adam Bede* and later in May became really enthusiastic about Charles Kingsley's life. 'C.K. imbues me with passing spirits of self-disgust and energy.' She also noted after the move to Lindsay Road: 'We discover that Glasnevin breezes inspire us with energy'.

By July 1911 Lucy had become more active in the suffrage movement. 'Have been at a great suffrage meeting and got badges, also got experiences. Quite carried away, as I afterwards relate to a sneerer. Today I get sore, wrathful and with some cause. I wish for strength to change (at least in my case) the condescending attitude of men towards our poor feeble wits.' In August she had a short holiday at Kingstown. 'Have had most enjoyable and rather exciting time. Boating and bathing.' She read *The Mill on the Floss* and wrote: 'It threatens almost to be-noodle me. I am carried away in a stream of sympathetic description, and live through nearly all fictitious experiences therein related.' Later, when Lucy read *Middlemarch,* she commented: 'I am at feet of George Eliot's shrine', which showed her intense admiration for both the content and style of this writer. She was also reading James Clarence Mangan and quoted him extensively in her diary.

On 7 January 1912 she joined the Irish Women's

Franchise League founded in 1908 by Hanna Sheehy Skeffington and Margaret Cousins, which was militant but non-party. On 21 May she noted that 'Elsie gets first number of new paper *Irish Citizen.*' This was the suffragist paper launched by Francis Sheehy Skeffington and James Cousins and for which Lucy later wrote articles.

Earlier the IWFL had commissioned Hopkins and Hopkins to make a replica of a Tara brooch for presentation to Mrs Pankhurst. It is possible that Elsie or Winnie may have suggested these silversmiths in view of the family connection with the firm.

CHAPTER EIGHT
1912–1913

Before continuing Lucy's personal saga, I will attempt a brief account of the events taking place in Dublin, though Lucy's preoccupations were her office work and suffrage activity.

There was acute poverty in the city with poor rates of pay for those who could find employment. James Larkin founded the Irish Transport and General Workers' Union in 1909 with the aim of securing better working conditions and higher wages for unskilled workers. The union grew quickly and in 1912 Larkin and James Connolly, who had been doing similar work in Belfast, founded the Irish Labour Party.

By 1913 employers became alarmed at the success of the ITGWU, so they formed their own organisation. An attempt to force their workers either to resign from the union or give a signed statement that they would not join it, precipitated a clash. A general strike and lockout followed in August 1913, which created great hardship and bitter feelings. It continued until early in 1914 when the workers were forced to return to work on the employers' terms. In November 1913 James Connolly and James White founded the Irish Citizen Army to protect workers in their clashes with police and this militia remained in existence.

The Third Home Rule Bill for Ireland was passed by the British legislature in 1912 and was due to come into law in 1914. The Ulster Volunteers were formed to resist this and the Irish Volunteers were set up in Dublin to defend it. A secret organisation called Irish Republican Brotherhood (successors to the earlier Fenians) infiltrated the Irish Volunteers hoping to promote a rebellion against British rule.

These events did not impinge directly on Lucy at this stage, as more personal matters developed.

During 1912 Samuel Kingston (Swik) occasionally invited Lucy to attend an opera with him and he found her 'so fascinating that she completed my infatuation and I definitely decided to win her if I could, in due time.' His caution arose out of the fact that Lucy had grown up with him as a part of the household until her family moved to Glasnevin in 1911. She regarded him as a good friend and almost as a brother and was at first unaware of his growing romantic interest in her.

Another difficulty facing Swik was the strongly militant view of suffrage Lucy then held. In June 1912 she noted: 'Swik comes and we argue hotly on suffrage—his criticism surprises me.'

Swik tried to show her his viewpoint by the following poem:

The Moralist and the Militants

A crash of breaking glass, a rush of feet,
A muttered imprecation, cheers, a scream,
A burst of mocking laughter—and the street
Seethes with a surging, struggling crowd who stream
Fast to the scene to see the latest fun—
A raid of Suffragettes has just begun!

Excited, nervous females, armed with stones
And hammers, work destruction all around.
They struggle with policemen—curses—groans—
And they are flung dishevelled on the ground.
The spectacle delights the jeering mob—
I turn away and stifle back a sob.

Yea, strong men wept for less—is this, O God,
What we have struggled up to from the past?—
Has Christ the path of love and suff'ring trod
That this should be the lesson learnt at last?—

'Throw Justice, Sense and Reason all away,
'Tis violence alone can win the day'!

We talk of progress and we dream of peace
And brotherhood and union, and we pray
The brute in Man may be worked out and cease—
But as we hope the Devil thus to lay,
Lo, he whom we have exorcised in Man
 Appears now in the woman hooligan!

Oh, Woman—thou who from the dawn of life
Hast stood the emblem of preserving love,
The type of peace, the enemy of strife,
The gentle angel pointing Man above—
Hast thou surrendered thy divinity,
Resolved to be as low a brute as he?

'Man won his freedom by brute force', you say
'So why not we'?—well, because that, my friends,
Good rose from evil, does not prove we may
Best use ill means to bring forth noble ends.
Else Principle's a lie and Christ's a fool
And gentleness is but the Devil's tool!

'Your wrongs'—Oh yes, I know your wrongs—
      disgrace—
How we have fed your body, starved your mind,
Prized you but as the breeder of the race
To give you freedom, knowledge, power, declined.
But why for this on Man put all the blame—
You acquiesced and gloried in your shame!

Ten thousand years obediently ye dwelt
Beneath Man's sway, and grew to love your chains,
Yea, forged them fresh—who more severely dealt
With rebels?—Who more loyal to your fanes,
Where 'with head covered' and 'forbid to speak'
As Man's inferiors ye sit every week!

Yet fifty years is far too long, forsooth,
To urge your claims and seek equality
With Man, reluctant to admit the truth
That Woman's sphere's not one of slavery.
Like peevish children ye impatient cry
And naught but violence will satisfy.

Know, 'tis not votes alone can make you free—
You must climb up the long and weary road
Of knowledge and experience patiently
You dallied—you must reap what you have sowed.
Blame, if you find your progress still is slow,
Not Man, but Providence that made it so!

With limitations ye are set around,
In many things as weaker must defer.
Of sex ye vainly strive to pass the bound,
And need not—Vast your sphere—ye greatly err
In imitating Man. Seek not his throne,
Rather enhance the glory of your own.

Oh, Woman—rouse thee from thy long neglect
Study, accomplish, reach thy destined goal,
Seek knowledge, freedom, culture, power, respect,
Yet ever be the gentle Woman-Soul—
But, bah—I speak to empty air alone—
A yell, a crash—there goes another stone!

S. W. K. 1912

Giving added point to their difficulties was a serious suffragette riot on 19 July in connection with Asquith's visit and an attempt to burn the Theatre Royal. Lucy was attacked by the mob going home that night as she was wearing a 'Votes for Women' badge and narrowly escaped by jumping on a passing tram. Swik was anxious about her safety after this.

Swik was a feminist in his upbringing (having grown up with four older sisters, the eldest of whom had helped to educate him and had been a financial support when his father's business had failed) and also in his conviction of the justness of women's demands for equal franchise. He wrote articles and spoke at meetings, but could not reconcile the militant angle with his regard for women and their potential. Lucy noted in October 1912 that she had attended a meeting at the Young Men's Christian Association at which there was a debate on militant suffrage activity. The votes cast were eight in favour of militancy and thirty-eight for conventional methods, and Lucy declined to vote. This was an important meeting in a personal sense, as Swik was one of the speakers against militancy, and the subsequent argument with Lucy caused him to have second thoughts about his courtship.

Swik was always a welcome visitor to Lucy's home but this gave no opportunity for privacy. He therefore used to meet her on Sunday evenings at Baggotrath Church after her choir duty and escort her home. They exchanged literary efforts, providing helpful criticism and encouragement to one another, and their friendship progressed steadily. However, the militancy issue again flared between them on 9 February 1913 and Swik was deeply torn, as he felt it a matter of principle that there should be no constraints upon the woman he married, 'and, moreover, I knew well Lucy would submit to no such restraint.' He therefore took Lucy's declaration that she had decided definitely in favour of militancy as a rupture and made no effort to see her for a month. He wrote in his diary 'Day and night, with brief intervals of distraction or stupor, the cursed question of militancy was running in my head—and the more so because I had promised to read a paper on "The Young Man's View of Women's suffrage" at the Dickens Fellowship meeting on 12 March, which Lucy had said she would attend and which I determined to make the cover for a last appeal to her reason and sentiment.'

Lucy wrote a note to Swik on 10 March, asking him to get his friend Herbert Buttimer to give herself and Dora Irish lessons, which Swik took as something in the nature of a flag of truce. Swik read his paper to quite a large audience, including Lucy, and next day had a chat with her which resulted in a complete reconciliation. She explained that she was annoyed at the imperious way in which Swik had questioned her on the night of the quarrel and so, in natural resentment, had exaggerated her advocacy of militancy. She said she was very doubtful of its principle or expediency, and was entirely opposed to some forms of it. They attended a Social Club whist drive and dance on 15 March, and Swik was thereafter happy and able to make up arrears of sleep!

The courtship continued but Lucy was also working hard at her singing as she won a silver medal for sight-reading at the Feis Ceoil and also won a gold medal for soprano singing. At this same Feis, Dora won gold and silver medals for contralto solo singing and for singing in Irish, of which she knew nothing, but both girls had been taught the pronunciation by Herbert Buttimer. Lucy was learning touch typing at work and also trying to become accustomed to use of the telephone. Strangely enough, she disliked the telephone all her life, but was quite at ease tapping out Morse code.

Finally Swik decided to end his long suspense by proposing to Lucy, but was unsure of how she would receive it as she expressed what he considered 'unromantic ideas on love and marriage' during discussions they had on feminism. He wrote a lengthy statement which he entitled 'A Psychological Proposal' in an attempt to deal with the intricacies of the situation. They went to see the rhododendrons in Howth on 21 June, and after tea strolled up the cliffs. There he presented his eight-page document.

In it he declared that his love for her was strong and

deep, but tried to make it clear that the friendship she expressed for him was not enough. He wrote:

You seem to dislike the word 'love'. To me, it is the best and noblest word in the language. Of course, I recognise that the ground of your objection is your exaggerated sex-prejudice. You fear that for the woman to give rein to her natural tenderness and romance is to give an opportunity for the man to put her in the subordinate position you so morbidly dread. I believe this to be a quite unfounded fear...I do not know that I can define love for you or analyse it. It includes romance, tenderness, loyalty, affection, unselfishness.'

He continued:

I do not expect passion from you. I must confess, indeed, that I would be human enough to welcome it if it were possible. But I am fully aware that I am very far from being an Adonis and cannot possibly hope to provoke passion in you, or in any woman. I cannot hope to have the same aesthetic value for you that you have for me. So I am content that any passion should be on my side. But this much I must ask for—that there should be sufficient sex-attraction to make my kisses at least not unwelcome to you...have dreamt a noble dream of a love between us that would be infinitely superior to friendship or affection or passion, that would be innately real and practical and not mere delusion, that would have the almost divine insight to see each other's faults and failings but to see through them with the spiritual sight that discerns the thoughts and intents of the heart...I have dreamt of a marriage in which we would be real lovers as well as real friends and comrades, free and equal so far as our limitations allow, helping, supporting, encouraging each other in work and aspirations and ideals, with minds and hearts in deep and strong sympathy…to realise the best that is in us, to acquire a wide and intense culture and to serve our generation so far as we have talent and opportunity.

We are both sensitive, egotistical, rather morbid, proud, strong-willed, devoted to principles and ideals, inclined to take ourselves very seriously and go to extremes, passionate though self-controlled. If we married merely on a basis of friendship and liking, we might get along together very well so long as our ideals and desires were in harmony. But when they differed, friction would be bound to arise that might make marriage a tragedy for us…On any basis of equality (and neither of us would submit to much subordination) the one and only force that could preserve harmony between a couple of such strong personality and sensitive nerves would be such a deep, strong, abiding, sympathetic love as I crave for.

He wound up by asking if she could love him like this, as he wanted all or nothing, and begged for a definite answer as soon as possible.

Lucy read it calmly, but with a deep flush on her cheek, and then informed him that she had taken his attentions only as platonic and was surprised (and disgusted) that he was human enough to fall in love. Swik wrote ruefully in his diary: 'It seemed she had regarded me as a sort of sexless superman.'

Lucy returned home that evening looking very disturbed and next day wrote in her diary: 'Howth yesterday with S. Revelations follow. Home before nine. La fin!' Within a few days she was on sick leave and confided in her mother, showing her the proposal. Sarah Anne wrote tactfully to Swik, and he called to see her alone on 22 August, when she disclosed Lucy's regret and gave him hope for the future. Lucy's only comment on this was: 'An old friend comes like a thief in the night to talk to Mammie, who commits breach of confidence.'

On 28 August Swik met Lucy at the GPO at 8 p.m. and saw her home. She explained that in her surprise she had spoken hastily at Howth but had reconsidered. By August 31 she wrote to him giving a definite acceptance and a declaration of love that more than satisfied Swik. Both families were informed and rings exchanged and Lucy complained in her diary that she was becoming sentimental!

CHAPTER NINE
1913–1915

Once they were engaged, the rest of the year seemed a happy and relaxed one for both Lucy and Swik. Lucy continued with her church choir singing and also joined Miss Culwick's Choir in October 1913. Here she sang until Miss Culwick's death in 1929. This choir is one of Ireland's longest established musical groups. It had its beginning as the Orpheus Choral Society, founded in 1898 by Dr J. C. Culwick, organist of the Chapel Royal, Dublin. When he died, his daughter Florence continued it, both as a ladies and a mixed choir. She attained high standards of performances up to her sudden death in 1929. The choir celebrated its seventy-fifth anniversary in 1973 and still continues as the Culwick Choral Society.

In July 1914 Lucy met Edward Harvey for the first time, Swik having referred to him warmly in his proposal as a sensitive friend. Lucy wrote: 'Met Edward Harvey. A man of seriousness very much unacquainted with humour. I like his discourse. We talk of woman's success in becoming eligible to elect on Church Councils—today's news.' It was fortunate that Lucy liked and respected Swik's friends. Edward and his brothers George and John lived in Rathmines Park. Edward had intended to be a clergyman, but then changed his mind and studied medicine, working in Baggot Street Hospital for many years.

Later in July Lucy paid her first visit to Skibbereen to meet Swik's family. She listed the various places visited in West Cork and her comment on the family was: 'Very favourably impressed. More so as each day passes with scenery, family powers of entertainment and qualities.'

Lucy's entry for 4 August 1914: 'Austria declares war on Serbia. Germany on Austria: later France on Germany: Russia joins in and England joins France to help fleet in protecting north coast of France. Pandemonium in office and all over Dublin and British Isles and Europe! General mobilisation within next few days. Ulster Volunteers are offered by Sir Edward Carson—later on National Volunteers and Ulster amalgamate and their own squabble sinks indefinitely.'

The outbreak of war greatly increased the pressures on the telegraph service. Lucy was doing eleven hours a day by August 6 and noted that the females had encroached on what was hitherto the men's monopoly of night duty. All messages were transmitted and received in Morse code on the newswire.

Swik wrote from Skibbereen suggesting a post-ponement of their wedding. This caused indignation in Lucy and her family as they felt such a suggestion should have come from her. However, when he returned he explained that there were now poor prospects in the Land Commission and that there would possibly be a shortage of work. Lucy understood his anxiety better but noted: 'Mammie and he discuss this while I hover in the kitchen, feeling rotten.' As they had arranged to purchase a newly built semi-detached house in Crescent Villas, Glasnevin in May, they postponed the wedding for only a month. Lucy left her office with many gifts and good wishes, feeling adrift as she had been employed for nearly eight years, almost six of them in the GPO. In those days women in the civil service were compelled to leave employment on marriage, so Lucy accepted the termination of this career without question.

The departmental magazine entitled *The Irish Postal and Telegraph Guardian* for October 1914 marked the occasion as follows:

Miss Lucy O. Lawrenson

We have much pleasure in presenting to our readers in this issue a photo of Miss Lawrenson, who on the 27th inst. entered the happy sphere of matrimony. Miss Lawrenson, during her sojourn in the Dublin office, worked steadily yet unobtrusively for the improvement of our conditions. In spheres outside the office she was well known for her work in connection with matters appertaining to the welfare of womankind. We have reason to know that in these spheres her genuine work and interest were as keenly appreciated as her efforts in the official circle. At the great meeting held in the Mansion House some months ago, presided over by the Lord Mayor, to protest against the findings of the Holt Report, Miss Lawrenson represented the female staff, and the excellent speech she delivered on the occasion delighted all who had the privilege of being present. We shall miss her kindly help and sound advice, and whilst regretting her departure we rejoice to think that the occasion is one of congratulation to her, and in saying that we wish her the best joy and happiness throughout the coming years, we do but in a small way voice the sentiments of every single member of the Dublin Telegraph Service.'

(The findings of the Report, commissioned in 1912 under the chairmanship of Frank Holt, dealt with rates of pay and cost of living allowances for Post Office workers, who were demanding higher rates to apply to Dublin as it was a more expensive place in which to live.)

There had been difficulties over the wedding ceremony itself as Swik and Lucy had considered being married in a registry office. Her mother's only references to the wedding were in November 1913 when she noted: 'Swik and Lucy thinking of Christmas twelve month, DV.', and a few days later: 'Unpleasantness with Lucy about Registry Office', and later again: 'Swik here in evening. Not too comfortable. Lucy and I at variance.'

Lucy felt she could not distress her mother further on the matter, so they discussed with the clergyman at St George's Church of Ireland whether he would agree to omit the word 'obey'. Despite considerable argument from both Lucy and Swik on the subject, they found the clergyman was adamant. The verbal account of the wedding I remember was that Lucy was furious at being forced to vow against her wishes and Swik was worried that the price of his bargain shoes would be visible to the congregation when he knelt! However, when I consulted their diaries for the actual day, it was nonchalantly reported by Lucy: '27 October 1914. The event today. S. and I stroll into George's and get hitched. Dora bridesmaid. Off to Warrenpoint by train where things run very pleasantly, smoothly and happily until our return. Walk ten miles daily. Liverpool Hotel a huge success.'

Swik's account was 'On Tuesday 27 October we were married in St George's Church by Rev K Dunlop, at 8.15 a.m., hiring a taxi for the occasion as the only extravagance in a very modest wedding. We got the 9 a.m. train to Warrenpoint and stayed there till 31st having splendid weather and a perfect time.' He wrote a poem there in which he playfully suggested that when he was a baby, four fairies had bestowed varied gifts which had left him prey to conflicts as an adult. He concluded: 'I need an Angel's help to guide—and lo—I find her by my side.'

They both accommodated themselves to double harness so quickly and well that they surprised themselves and their relations. Lucy handled the unaccustomed and uncongenial business of housekeeping well. Swik marvelled at his surpassing good fortune and claimed that his 'idiotic happiness' was a source of complaint with Lucy!

By November 1914 Lucy had promised to do some office routine at the Irishwomen's Reform League and thereafter became more and more involved with their work. This League was formed in Dublin as one of the organisations under the umbrella of the Irish Women's Suffrage Federation established by Louie Bennett and Helen Chenevix. Lucy was asked by Miss Chenevix to act as secretary of literature for the Reform League and appointed to the consultative committee of the *Irish Citizen*. Her early interest in extensive reading and in writing a wide range of articles was stimulated and encouraged by Swik, both before and after their marriage. Release from her office work enabled her to devote time to writing, and during 1915 she was a frequent contributor to the *Irish Citizen*. She wrote a number of serious articles such as 'The Suffragette and the War', 'Some Lessons of 1914' and 'Feminine Bosses'. In another called 'Handicaps' she suggested that a modern St Paul would have brought his words up to date and would have sounded less repressive of women. She wrote a series of three light-hearted articles under the general title of 'Our Home Enemies', listing them as Fashions, War Germs and Snobbery. She also contributed two long articles on 'Economic Foundation of the Women's Movement'.

Swik had undertaken an Arts degree course at National University (having found he was eligible as an old Royal University of Ireland extern student) and was studying hard for this. When any difficulties or tensions arose between them, they talked them through and Lucy frequently noted in her diary: 'Nous nous comprenons', occasionally adding the words, 'très bien.' She maintained great reserve in her diary, using occasional French phrases or shorthand to make personal comments.

Life continued busily and happily for them both until March 1915 when they heard that Daisy, Swik's beloved eldest sister, who had married Tom Mansfield of Cappoquin in 1913, had died in childbirth, after the added complication of pneumonia, and that the child was stillborn. Swik was deeply grieved and sought solace in writing poetry. Lucy felt puzzled and pained by the suffering involved.

On 27 April she noted: 'Six months married and still cheerful.' and on 1 June: 'Twenty-three years and nothing done.' However, she was playing tennis and when she and Swik went to Portmarnock to bathe she managed sixty-two strokes!

Lucy regularly attended the Irishwomen's Reform League meetings and there heard of the proposal to hold an International Women's Conference in The Hague that summer. She reported hot debates taking place as to whether Ireland should be represented and commented, 'Mrs Sheehy Skeffington very good and non-party.' Miss Louie Bennett attended the Hague Congress, and within a few months she suggested to Lucy that an Irish section should be formed. Mrs Helena Swanwick, well-known in Britain as a suffragist and labour leader, addressed a meeting in Sackville Hall in October and an Irish section of the Women's International League was formed. For many years Lucy was involved in committee meetings and frequently served as secretary or as chairperson of the Irish section. She took a keen interest in the work at its headquarters in Geneva of the Women's International League for Peace and Freedom (as it later became).

During 1915 she was writing further articles for the *Irish Citizen*, and on 14 September she received the following postcard:

> Irish Women's Franchise League,
> Westmoreland Chambers,
> Westmoreland Street,
> Dublin.

> Now that *Irish Citizen* has returned to its ordinary size (eight pages) we shall be most grateful for articles or sketches. Your 'Conversational Snatches' held over owing to lack of space appears this week. It is delightful—every line of it. Please send us as much as you can!

> H. S. Skeffington (Acting Editor).

This was one part of a three-part series poking gentle fun at the type of arguments women produced among themselves when discussing feminism. She cited a matron saying patronisingly to her, 'Wait until you are married, then you will view it differently', to which Lucy replied with some satisfaction, 'But I am!'

The description 'acting editor' was because Francis (Hanna's husband) had been arrested and sentenced to six months hard labour for an 'anti-recruiting' speech. Francis was a committed pacifist as well as feminist, and his courage and outspokenness frequently brought him into conflict with the authorities.

CHAPTER TEN
1916–1918

In March 1916 Lucy entered in her diary: 'Teeming day. I resolve to write a novel 'when I grow up' which will enlighten humanity re certain psychological puzzles in feminine experiences of life!' Alas, this resolve was overtaken by dramatic events in Dublin the following month.

The Rising which took place at Easter 1916 was planned by the Supreme Council of the Irish Republican Brotherhood. Meanwhile, James Connolly and the Irish Citizen Army were planning their own rebellion, but were persuaded to join with the IRB. Eoin MacNeill was the leader of the Irish Volunteers but discovered the plan for the Rising only on 20 April (Holy Thursday). Roger Casement's attempt to import arms failed so Eoin MacNeill cancelled all Volunteer activities for Easter Sunday. The IRB decided to proceed on Easter Monday and captured many important buildings, making the GPO their headquarters. It had been a well-kept secret as even Margaret Pearse, mother of the IRB leader, Padraig Pearse, learnt of the plan only on the eve of Easter Monday.

From Lucy's very detailed day-by-day account (in red ink) in her diary one can glean how the Easter Rising must have seemed to the ordinary citizen who was subject to constant rumours and taken completely by surprise at the eruption of a rebellion in the middle of the 1914-18 war.

Lucy and Swik had spent Easter Monday, 24 April, cycling at Glendalough and, while returning on a delayed train from Rathdrum, heard rumours re: 'Sinn Féiner doings in Dublin.' They reached Glasnevin safely but heard shooting during the night. Next day they found that the gas had been turned off and that there was no post or newspapers. There were rumours that shops were being looted all over the city. They heard intermittent firing and everyone was discussing the matter on their doorsteps. There were rumours that Sinn Féiners had also taken control of Cork, Waterford and Limerick.

On the third day Liberty Hall was bombarded from the river. A military proclamation asked people to keep within doors but this was totally disregarded. Liam Harrison (Dora's fiancé) reported that his family's studio in Sackville Place had been gutted and all furniture and musical instruments destroyed.

By Thursday rumours were intensifying. When Lucy went to search unsuccessfully for bread she was told that James Connolly had been shot and that Constance Markievicz was to be shot that day. She was also told of Roger Casement's imprisonment in the Tower and of the plot which failed and which proved the excuse for this uprising. She heard that 'Skeffy' had urged the Sinn Féins to form a police force to go around the city and stop the looting: best idea so far, as looters are going ahead all over the city and no shop is safe.' Shops sold their supplies of food by allowing only a few customers at a time entrance through barred gates. Money and rations were running a bit short everywhere. The military had sealed off the centre of Dublin from the north side by placing checkpoints on every bridge over the Royal Canal, so all male citizens had to apply for a pass before being allowed across.

Their neighbour Ned Jones told them that it was not safe to show a light at the back of houses as the military were suspicious of lights and signals: 'Different rumours about great fire last night,' was one of Friday's entries. There were reports of battles on Rialto Bridge and a neighbour had to ride his bicycle with his pass in his mouth for fear of military shooting. Sniping went on all through the day but not much serious shooting.

On Saturday there was less and less food to be had and denser crowds outside the shops. It was rumoured that Sheehy Skeffington had tried to organise a police force and had been arrested and shot. 'Resolve to spy out the road to Belfast in case of shortage of food and in view of rumours re looting which is suspected from the starving mob.' A British Army officer being entertained by a neighbour commented 'France is a picnic in comparison with this!' Later that day they were 'electrified with the news from several people that all is over and a surrender made. Sceptical.'

On Sunday at church the boom of guns in the distance contrasted strangely with the hymn 'Peace, Perfect Peace.' 'Doubtful as to peace even yet, but the general explanation seems true, that a small force (two hundred) having surrendered, those away from the centre have not heard of this and are fighting and holding out, individually, apart from their leadership, according as their valour dictates.'

On Monday 1 May Lucy heard that women in search of bread were allowed over one bridge so she went down to Sackville Street. 'Awful desolation. The front wall of Clery's stands up like a bulwark, GPO is a shell, many houses have disappeared, several feet high of debris lies in Henry Street and altogether the sight is appalling.' Later that day Swik and Lucy tried to get a pass for him 'when we observe the evolutions of militarism (futile and silly) for two long hours.' Finally Swik lost his place in the long queue and after he had failed to regain it (by reason partly of his Cork accent) they gave up in despair.

On Tuesday there was more frustration over obtaining a pass (there seemed to be positive discrimination in favour of women as only men needed passes) and she commented: 'More fooling and blundering. Pass system a nuisance. Tired of English jargon.'

By Thursday 4 May various offices resumed their work. There was no further news about Sheehy Skeffington but Lucy began to believe the rumour must be true, although there was no account of his trial. Martial law remained in force and passes were still necessary.

By Saturday 6 May 'normality' reigned once more but 'rebel leaders' were being shot daily or sentenced to imprisonment. 'No fixed news about Skeffington yet but think he has gone. Eight gone so far. Many tales emerge, some true, some false. Last night I got hold of Sinn Féin pamphlet (explaining policy) which I read and then burned.' By Tuesday 9 May Lucy wrote 'Miserable days! Executions taking place daily. Markievicz sentenced to death, commuted to life servitude. Plunkett gone. Skeffy buried yesterday.'

One can sense Lucy's shift of opinion during these sixteen days of confusion. At first she and her family were just surprised at the rebellion and dismayed at its effects on the ordinary citizens, but slowly the felt a desire to understand and finally there was real distress at the executions. As she had worked with both Francis and Hanna Sheehy Skeffington on the paper *Irish Citizen*, Lucy was particularly shocked that Francis had been killed.

On 20 May Lucy went to the Irish Women's Franchise League for a committee meeting in connection with the *Irish Citizen* fund and debt. 'Memorial number (to Francis Sheehy Skeffington) to be brought out when martial law is removed. Much hot discussion. I am put on committee, alas! Much disgusted with the logic of the IWFL. Come to the conclusion that the IWFL is "the Skeffys" and without them it is simply talk and fanaticism.' Lucy never had any desire to be drawn into politics and was more interested in peace and women's social concerns.

In August Lucy and Swik went to Skibbereen for a holiday and enjoyed visiting the various beauty spots in the area.

On 25 March 1917 Lucy noted: 'I stay in all day for first time since October 27, 1914! Studious day.' Both Swik and Lucy read extensively and were deeply interested in religious and current affairs. A Quaker influence was Eileen Hawker who had been a lodger in Rathmines in 1902 and had established a friendship with the family.

Lucy later visited an elderly friend of her mother, Annie Sidney Eustace, who lived in Glasnevin. She was a rather delicate but strong-minded woman who had joined the Quakers from the Church of Ireland. Lucy was impressed by these two women and came to realise that women held an equal position within the Society of Friends, both in their worship and business affairs. The Quaker position on pacifism and their support for conscientious objectors also appealed to her as the war continued. She began to attend the Quaker meetings in Rathmines. Through them she became friendly with Gertrude Webb, another older woman who had considerable influence on her.

Both she and Swik were stimulated by the sermons delivered for so many years by Reverend Saville Hicks and visiting speakers at the Unitarian Church on St Stephen's Green.

They went to the Abbey Theatre frequently, occasionally to the Gaiety, and also took up whist. In season they played tennis vigorously, gardened (growing their own potatoes and other vegetables) and Swik enjoyed playing hockey. They walked and cycled both on a daily basis and on holiday. Lucy enjoyed very good health but Swik suffered from many ailments all during his life, which he attributed to being over-protected and spoilt by his mother when a very young child! She had been so overjoyed to have a son after four girls and one son who died in infancy that he was almost 'killed by kindness.' His younger brother was a much hardier specimen, and lived to the age of ninety.

There was always close contact between the Kingston couple and the household run by Sarah Anne, to which many family relations called. Many also stayed overnight when up from County Wicklow.

On 28 March 1917 Lucy's entry was 'A great day for Suffs. Mr Wait-and-See' [H. H. Asquith] 'announces his support of women's suffrage yesterday in House. Bill recognized by speakers conference to apply to Ireland.'

The Representation of the People Bill, giving the vote to women over thirty years of age, was passed in January 1918. In the enfranchisement number of *Englishwoman* magazine published in March 1918 Lucy had an article entitled 'An Irishwoman's Outlook' which was a cool appraisal of the Irish scene. In it she pointed out that the news of the passing of The Representation of the People Bill would be quietly received as the Home Rule question had divided support for franchise reform. She felt that the thorny Irish political situation had given rise to more suffrage societies than were essential and tended to divide rather than unite. Some would continue to fight for complete franchise, while others would turn to social reform and educative work. She felt that the emergence of Sinn Féin had provided a real alternative for voters. She feared that women would, like men, tend to use their votes in a party political way but thought there would be more support for women candidates for municipal and poor law elections. To the thinking Irishwoman, the giving of the vote was less of a feeling of triumph in a victory, than a natural feeling of pride in the (partial) recognition that the stigma hitherto placed on the woman citizen was an injustice and a mistake.

A brief return to Swik's diary expands a cryptic note of Lucy's in June 1917: 'Decide on change in menage.' He wrote 'On June 21—the fourth anniversary of 'putting the question'—Lucy and I had a frank discussion on our domestic arrangements and decided to undertake the full duties—and privileges—of matrimony, a decision so important that it constitutes the event of the year for us.'

They were clearly practising intentional family planning but the form it took is not revealed. In fact, Lucy was almost as reserved as her mother about pregnancy, as on 27 August she noted: 'S., a witch, finds out that which it is not yet necessary for him to know.' She had had, of course, many comments during the years on her freedom from ties and in October noted 'Miss Bennett quizzes me about my "unfettered" condition', but now can add to her diary with glee '(just you wait a bit, Louisa!)' She continued her various committees for the rest of 1917, but gradually retired from them in the early part of 1918 and on May 12 her first child was born.

Swik's description was 'I spent a very anxious fortnight in May, complicated by fears of anti-conscription riots, till the time came for Lucy to go into Mrs Gavan's Nursing Home in North Frederick Street—on the night of Friday 10 May, and after a weary wait I learned the glad tidings on Sunday afternoon, 12 May, that Lucy was all right and that I was the father of a son—henceforth to be loaded with the name of Ralph William Lawrenson Kingston. I was not free from a measure of old-fashioned pride in finding him a healthy, vigorous baby, without spot or blemish, quite a eugenic success! Lucy was very weak at first, but pulled up well and was able to come home on May 25.' This would seem an incredible length—and expense—of hospitalisation for most modern women but presumably it was customary then, at least for first babies. Lucy's subsequent children were born at home. In early June she noted: 'I have to definitely give up nursing as haven't the right sort of constitution. Very disappointed.'

Sarah Anne was, of course, delighted at the birth of her first grandchild and must have been especially touched that he should be called Ralph. However, there were difficulties between herself and Lucy on the matter of having him baptised. As has been shown earlier, Lucy had been attracted to the Quaker Meeting in Rathmines and was interested in their different view of the sacraments. She had ceased her paid singing in church choirs and had become increasingly dismayed by what she termed 'recruiting speeches' rather than sermons during the war years. She therefore did not wish Ralph to be baptised into the Church of Ireland but met with deep disapproval from her family. On 21 June she wrote: 'Get messages from Mr Greening [clergyman] by Winnie which opens up subject of baptism for I hope last time.' In Sarah Anne's diary were the comments 'Elsie and Lucy had it out about baptism.' and 'Up very early to Lucy and she and I had another talk on baptism.' Lucy's comment on this interview was 'Mammie and I still at daggers drawn about christening so resolve to see Miss Edith Webb if possible tomorrow. Unable to see Miss Webb so write her instead and get in return long letter and book on Quaker position and sacraments which give to Mammie.'

Quakers, from the earliest teachings of their founder George Fox in the 1650s, always put emphasis on the spiritual aspect of the sacraments and believed that to stress the outward symbols was to distract from the inner meaning. They therefore dispensed with outward forms of baptism, confirmation, communion and set rituals of service, asserting the positive truth that the religious life is the inward life of the spirit and that all can have direct experience without the need for intermediaries.

Having given in to her mother on the subject of her wedding, Lucy now seemed determined to be independent in her stand on baptism. She continued to attend Quaker meetings for worship and learned more about their methods of conducting their business affairs, the democracy and equality of the sexes appealing greatly to her. In the early 1920s she joined the Religious Society of Friends (Quakers). Sarah Anne must have become reconciled to the idea, but Winnie, however, always regarded Lucy as a renegade in this regard. Swik was sympathetic but at this stage was more drawn to the Unitarian Church (which they both attended frequently) and did not join the Quakers until the early 1930s, when he and the three children were accepted into membership.

The last few chapters have not referred to the progress of the war raging in Europe, but there were numerous references to current news of battles in both Sarah Anne's and Lucy's diaries. Apart from one first cousin of Lucy's from Ballinglen, Joey Boyd, who fought throughout and survived, and some much older Lawrenson first cousins, their immediate relatives were not involved, but Swik and Lucy were deeply concerned and increasingly disillusioned.

In addition to his full-time work in the Land Commission, Swik sat for his B.A. examination, and his degree was conferred in July 1916. He then began making splints for the Red Cross, took up first aid lectures and bandaging classes in his office and subsequently joined the St John's Ambulance Brigade. In 1917 he went through a long course of ambulance drill, got a full khaki uniform in April, and was declared fit for stretcher bearing at North Wall, where ambulances met hospital ships bringing back the wounded. He used to tell with wry amusement of his embarrassment on being seized by an emotional woman and hearing her say almost with tears, 'Oh, you good brave man, was it dreadful out there?'

About this time Lucy joined the Fellowship of Reconciliation and attended their meetings frequently. This was a Christian pacifist group formed in England at the beginning of the 1914 war for the reconciliation of Europe and the world. A Dublin branch was started in 1915, one of its first members being Helen Chenevix, and Gertrude Webb was honorary secretary. The group tried to offer support to the families of those executed or imprisoned after the 1916 Rising and also kept contact with English conscientious objectors who had been transferred to Irish prisons. Lucy remained a member until the branch disbanded in 1921.

In July 1918 there was the first mention of the 'influenza' epidemic and again in October of that year, but none of the family caught the infection.

The Armistice was signed on 11 November 1918 and that terrible war abroad came to an end, but political events were coming to a head in Ireland.

Britain had regarded the 1916 Rising as a Sinn Féin rebellion and the organisation's leader, Arthur Griffith, was placed under arrest. Though not directly involved in the Rising, Sinn Féin had benefitted from being associated with the executed leaders and the party grew steadily. In October 1917 Eamon de Valera, who had been imprisoned after the 1916 Rising, took over the leadership of the new Sinn Féin and the Volunteers.

In the General Election held in December 1918, out of 106 seats, Sinn Fein won seventy-three, the Unionists twenty-six and the Irish parliamentary party only six. The Sinn Féin Members of Parliament refused to attend the Westminster parliament and in January 1919 formed their own parliament known as the First Dáil. In April de Valera was elected President and appointed ministers, among whom was Constance Markievicz as Minister for Labour. The British government declared Sinn Féin and the Dáil to be illegal. At the same time the War of Independence began.

CHAPTER ELEVEN
1919–1921

Early in 1919 both Lucy and Swik frequently attended Esperanto classes and Lucy joined the League of Nations group. However, by 20 February she had contracted the influenza that had reached epidemic proportions and Swik had a very anxious and busy time for a week nursing her and minding Ralph. He got half-days off from the office. Lucy was by then able to sit up and was convalescent by the beginning of March, though weak and shaken in health for long afterwards.

On 3 March members of the household at 'Mirtna' got influenza and Swik heard that his brother Willie was also down with a bad attack in Skibbereen. He wrote: 'Anxiety was piled on anxiety. I escaped the infection myself by constant use of quinine, aspirin and lysol gargling etc. Elsie developed pneumonia and we moved her to Drumcondra Hospital on 6 March, where she died on March 12. Her death, needless to say, came as a great shock and sorrow to me as to all of us. I took three days leave to help in the funeral arrangements and was busy for some time after in arranging administration to her effects.'

This influenza was also called 'Spanish flu' or 'trench fever' and took a terrible toll, especially in the Dublin area. On 13 March Lucy wrote: 'I go down to get my mourning at Holmes and there meet Winnie Ormsby, widowed yesterday' and next day commented that she was appalled at the losses all round. On 16 March her entry noted: 'Mammie looks badly to-day and her hair has turned snow white.' Elsie's death was a great sorrow for them all, but a crushing blow for Sarah Anne as Elsie was a wonderfully steady character and was a constant companion and close friend of her mother. Swik attempted to comfort her by composing a poem which Dora illuminated.

On 31 March Lucy noted: 'Europe starving these days, yet the Allies continue to blockade Germany for the good of her soul. Hungary went Bolshevik by the consent of the cabinet a few days ago. The chief enemy of the Allies now is Bolshevism, to fight which they would willingly ally with reactionary section in Germany!! A complete turnabout! Yet they continue to starve and freeze the German people!' In April Lucy wrote: 'Take over with quakings the custody of Irish Famine Fund—it is at any rate a piece of direct work in the preservation of our crumbling civilisation'. This fund was established by the Irishwomen's International League and Lucy wrote an article on it for the *Irish Citizen*.

The disastrous beginning of 1919 was compensated for later in the year by Swik and Lucy, who took Ralph with them for a successful holiday in West Cork in July. In December Lucy had her first visit to London. She and Swik went for ten days over Christmas, leaving Ralph in the charge of Sarah Anne and her sister Janie. They greatly enjoyed doing 'the sights' with Dick Mansfield, stepson of Swik's sister Daisy, a gentle literary man then living in London.

Lucy originally started to learn Irish because she wished to enter the Feis Ceoil competition for singing in Irish. However, her interest was maintained and her entry for 29 February 1920 reads: 'Buttimer and I do Irish in garden. After dinner Swik and I go to Botanic bringing Ralph who makes friends with all and sundry. These are disturbed days in Ireland which I must not forget to recount. Raids every other night, shootings, thefts and murders in England also. Curfew order in force since last Monday. When will our Irish class in which am greatly interested be also prohibited?'

In the early months of 1920 law and order were breaking down. Michael Collins had reorganised the

Volunteer movement which, as the Irish Republican Army, used the tactic of guerrilla warfare: small groups carrying out surprise attacks on the British forces and withdrawing quickly. To combat these tactics, the British sent over a new force of unemployed ex-soldiers who wore a uniform of dark green and khaki and became known as the Black and Tans. A smaller force, the Auxiliaries, comprising ex-army officers, was sent in August 1920 and both groups were given great freedom to terrorise both the IRA and the civilian population.

Lucy's diary on Easter Monday 5 April 1920 reads: 'Hear this morning eighty barracks attacked all over the country and thirty-five burned. Frightful anarchy and disturbance.' On 11 April: 'Go to Irish Service at 5 p.m. which is rather good. Awful crowds outside Mountjoy Prison and hunger-strikers (a hundred) at their last gasp. Great excitement.' On April 13: 'General strike on account of prisoners not being released. They are in a very weak and dangerous condition—Dublin in a dangerous condition too though not weak. About ten or twelve thousand people assemble at Mountjoy Prison and shout from two till ten o'clock.' She continued on 14 April: 'All shops still shut and strike goes on. Stop Press comes that prisoners are released—great rejoicings outside prison and Unionist indignation, although *The Irish Times* is very moderate and English papers approve of government's action.'

The *Irish Times* related on 12 April 1920 that crowds of sympathisers had gathered outside the prison gates the day before, and that their numbers grew so large that the military were ordered to move in to keep people away from the prison. The military remained on duty for the rest of the day and night (one soldier was wounded by discharging his own revolver). On 13 April, *The Irish Times* leader page had an article entitled 'A Plea for Sanity', calling for clemency, and the Lord Mayor and High Sheriff appealed for intervention. Lucy's account of the hours of civilian shouting seems an interesting example of passive resistance not documented elsewhere.

As well as being in charge of the Famine Fund mentioned earlier, Lucy and Swik felt they should offer to take an undernourished European temporarily into their home. Lucy had heard of such a scheme through her membership of the Fellowship of Reconciliation. In September 1920 she and Swik went to North Wales for a short holiday and on their way back met by arrangement Anna Kapler, a young Austrian, who lived with them until February 1921. She and Lucy formed a friendship and corresponded for some years afterwards, Anna subsequently sending her wedding photograph.

In November 1920 Buttimer escorted Lucy to a concert given by the Carl Rosa Company in La Scala Theatre. There was a row afterwards with her mother because the music was not sacred and the day was Sunday! Lucy noted in her diary: 'Fed-up.' Even six years after Lucy had left home, Sarah Anne attempted to impose her own standards of behaviour!

On 21 November Lucy noted: 'Bad Sunday. Eleven officers assassinated (court martial men) and afterwards twelve people killed and sixty wounded at Croke Park football match. Shots heard here. People dazed over the events. Dublin put under 10 o'clock curfew (the worst in our experience since Rebellion) and in a state of great unrest. Black and Tans pervade the place.' The IRA had killed men believed to be British intelligence agents and the Black and Tans took revenge by opening fire at a crowded Gaelic football match the same afternoon.

Dublin became more and more disturbed during 1921 and Lucy mentioned ambushes during the early months of the year. There was a military raid on the offices of the *Irish Citizen* in which the office was wrecked. This put an end to the paper. Curfew hours became earlier, to Lucy's great indignation. Ordinary people took risks in order to carry on their social lives: they were in danger of being shot while so doing.

In April Willie Kingston and his sister Rachel came by train to Dublin as there had been many cases of random killings of Protestant men in West Cork. Willie was a solicitor in Skibbereen and feared he might be a target; his cousin and partner Jasper Wolfe had temporarily left the country after a threat. Willie emigrated and took a position with a firm of solicitors in South Africa, but found he was uncomfortable about the growing apartheid system, so he returned to Ireland when the Troubles subsided.

From 1914 to 1925 Edward and Frances Jones were next-door neighbours of Lucy's at Crescent Villas and a friendship developed which lasted until Frances's death in 1954. Both women suffered miscarriages and their children were born around the same time. A typical comment of Lucy's in May 1921 shows the pleasant relationship: 'To tea at 24. Mrs Jones very confidential this time. We talk over broken friendships and deplore the sure on-creeping of old age'—they were around twenty-nine years of age! They also had similar musical tastes and Lucy gave a ticket for the Feis to Mrs Jones: 'She hears Fantaisie in F Minor and other pieces for Pigott Memorial Cup. She comes in very enthusiastic about it and illustrates on piano.'

Around this time Lucy formed another long-lasting friendship with Helen Chenevix. Helen and Louie Bennett had been early members of the suffrage movement and Lucy worked closely with both on the Reform League and the International League. Through her Lucy met others such as Ruby Holt and her daughter Betty, and also Helen Lloyd. All these women expanded her network of contacts, especially when she moved from the north to the south side of Dublin.

Early in June 1921 Lucy and Rosamund Jacob were appointed Irish delegates to the Congress in Vienna of the Women's International League, which seemed so important to Lucy in its encouragement to women to work internationally for peace and freedom. Lucy had not even met Rose at this stage, as family matters had detained Rose in Waterford for some time. They corresponded over passport matters but met for the first time only on 21 June and Lucy noted: 'Like her very much.' They attended the congress from 5 July to 21 July, and established a firm friendship which lasted until Rose's death in 1960. Rose's brother Tom and his wife Dorothea Farrington were also very popular guests in the Kingston household.

While Lucy was away in Vienna the truce between British and Irish forces was declared at noon on 11 July, after which tension was much relaxed and something like pre-war conditions were restored. The subsequent treaty negotiations continued until 6 December. On that date the Treaty was signed, with the twenty-six counties given dominion status as a member of the British Commonwealth under the title of the Irish Free State.

A more personal event marked the end of the year as Lucy, after about three months' pregnancy, had a miscarriage in early December and both she and Swik were depressed for some time after this.

CHAPTER TWELVE
1922–1924

1922 was a very disturbed year in Irish politics. Early in the year Swik, who was anxious about his position as a civil servant under the old regime, wrote: 'Great political excitement. Treaty approved by Dáil on 7 January by a bare majority of seven and formally ratified on 14 January. Provisional Government being then set up. Final British Treasury award hurriedly issued on January 14 as to Land Commission's clerks' sssimilation terms. I only got two £7/10/0. increments, very disappointing after all our agitation and very unjust—but protests unavailing. With a view to the future, I now took up the study of Irish again, but in desultory and half-hearted fashion.'

Following the close vote on the Treaty, de Valera resigned, objecting to the oath of allegiance. Michael Collins and Arthur Griffith were strongly pro-Treaty. The Free State government, with Arthur Griffith as its President, proceeded to take over from the British, who were withdrawing from the country.

The IRA were bitterly divided, with one faction becoming absorbed into a new national army, and another ready to take up arms against the Treaty. These became known as the Irregulars and occupied the Four Courts under Rory O'Connor in April 1922.

An election was held in June 1922 but this increased the bitterness. Michael Collins ordered the Free State army to shell the Four Courts and the Civil War began. It lasted until April 1923.

Lucy and Swik's sister, Sarah Peard, were making enquiries about a holiday in the Isle of Man. Then Lucy noted on 28 June: 'Battle last night—Four Courts attacked by Free State troops, it is thought at the instigation of Churchill who demands stronger action on the part of

Free State or else they will repudiate Treaty—but this motive afterwards denied by Free State. Shooting goes on all day.' Next day she commented that big guns were still pounding away at Four Courts. 'Business at standstill and housewives out foraging for food, myself included. Sleepless and anxious nights and days.' On 30 June she wrote: 'Swik goes down to-day but runs great risk. Tremendous explosion occurs at about 12 o'clock. It is a mine exploding in Four Courts and fifty Free Staters are blown up but none fatally. At 3.30 the surrender takes place and Four Courts goes up in flames—another fine building gone. Looting of shops takes place, but Free Staters threaten to shoot looters on sight. Offer of help from British troups rejected. Ralph and Elizabeth do not mind the guns which is a blessing. We are relieved from distant pounding since Four Courts went up, but sniping and constant rifle-shots pretty bad around us. Roads near Bray trenched and a bridge blown up. Louie Bennett, Miss Ryan and another have petitioned Minister of Defence to have women and children in danger zone allowed to take over empty houses, also to have food supplies secured. We look to Isle of Man as to a haven of rest away from sound of guns—will we ever get there!'

On 3 July Lucy noted: 'Skibbereen fighting has broken out, also Cork. Whole thing seems useless bloodshed, ruin and destruction to trade.' On July 24 they did get away for a refreshing holiday in the Isle of Man which cost only £16 for the three Kingstons for the entire month, including travel. They were shocked on their return by news of the death of Michael Collins, following so soon on the death of Arthur Griffith. On 10 September Swik's sister Rachel arrived (by boat from Cork as many rail bridges had been blown up) bringing family scrip certificates and papers which Swik kept for safety, such was the disturbed state of West Cork at that time.

On 13 September Lucy had another miscarriage which she feared might have been brought on by a long walk.

From left, Elsie, Winnie, Lucy, Dora after the move to Dublin, 1897

Sarah Anne Lawrenson in the early 1900s

Lucy, Ralph and Sarah Anne, two months after Elsie's death in 1919

Swik in 1908

Lucy aged twenty-one in 1913 wearing Feis Ceoil gold medal

Annelies, Daisy, Elsa at Sorrento greenhouse about 1935

Lucy in 1964, aged 72

They were very disappointed and Lucy wrote: 'Swik and I try Couéism, prompted by a book of Bevins!! It is all that we can do.' Emile Coué, a French pharmacist, had become interested in hypnosis and then evolved his own simple system of auto-suggestion. He wrote and lectured on the subject and his slogan, 'Every day in every way, I am getting better and better,' was much in vogue around this time.

All during these worrying times, Herbert Buttimer was giving recitals of his gramophone records, which was very relaxing, and Lucy noted that he had then 230 records in all. Earlier in the year, Willie Kingston had returned from South Africa at the urgent request of his sisters, but against Swik's better judgment. On 11 October Lucy noted 'Willie sails this morning under smiling skies. Situation here fully justifies his going away again as it gets worse and more dangerous than ever and though emigration wave ebbs, yet it looks as if we would all be well advised to flit.'

On 2 November: 'Go to general meeting Irishwomen's International League. Great turnout (for us). Miss Bennett definitely gives up secretaryship. Also gives us a warning about employing on committee etc. women who take prominent place in contemporary politics.' Lucy and her committee members had always tried to keep Irish internal politics out of the International League.

On 17 November Swik and Lucy attended the Dáil to hear Irish Land Commission debate and heard most of the ministers speak. Lucy continued: 'Four executions to-day which starts the new regime of military courts so we may look out for squalls.'

Lucy's first entry for 1923 was on 2 January: 'Ralph's first day at school, relieved and at same time experiencing the usual parents' feelings at the first emptying of the nest (occupied by one!) Exciting news about Rose Jacob. I go to committee at her flat at 4 o'clock and find she is under arrest since Saturday in consequence of having agreed to lend part of Mrs Sheehy Skeffington's house to republican publicity department in Mrs Skeffington's stead. Think her action was what Mrs S. S. would have agreed to, but considering Rose's position as secretary to the Irishwomen's International League rather rash, as from our point of view we are not benefitted in any way by having our secretary in prison. Madame Gonne MacBride reports she tried to see Rose at Portobello Barracks during weekend, failed, and afterwards finds she is in Mountjoy. We agree that if possible we should see Mulcahy and urge that her case be tried soon. Mrs Johnson, self, Miss Bennett and Mrs Dix deputed for job. Very glad we have Mrs Dix as joint secretary—she is a sane and thoroughly pacifist person and does not stink in eyes of government like Mrs Despard and Madame Gonne MacBride. Question of Mrs Despard's resignation arises again but she declared herself a pacifist and "neutral" in the eyes of the government.' Lucy discussed this proposed deputation with Swik that night and he explained that it might reflect on his position in civil service so Lucy agreed not to go. Later it was agreed not to send the deputation.

Rose Jacob was always interested in Sinn Féin and took a republican stand during the Civil War, as did Madame Gonne MacBride and Mrs Despard. The Free State government kept a close watch on republican sympathisers and pounced upon Rose when she lent part of Mrs Sheehy Skeffington's house while caretaking in her absence. This was an example of what Louie Bennett had foreseen and warned about in the previous November when she resigned from the secretaryship of the Irishwomen's International League.

Lucy had more personal problems on her mind. '5 January. Go to doctor with my tale today, keeping Mrs Langan till 3.30 as do not want to explain my journey to 'Mirtna'. Find him very sympathetic and quite understands my apprehensions in view of latest events— anxieties and fears actually dog me this time and I make absolutely no preparations or plans, and have no hopes for going full time. Watching myself every hour, to the possible permanent destruction of my mental health and sane outlook!' Having had two miscarriages fairly recently, Lucy was very keen to go full term this time, but feared hypocondria!

In February Lucy's preoccupations were with the political state of the country. 'Mansions going all over the country', and she lists the large numbers of houses burnt in and around Dublin. On 29 March Swik noted: 'I bade farewell to the Belfast contingent in the office on the last day of the British regime. We were handed over to the Free State on March 31. In view of the disturbed state of the country I had seriously considered going to Belfast with the Land Commission but finally decided to trust my fortunes to Saorstát. I did some half-hearted study of Irish, but had not time or energy to do it properly.' Before very long, their decision to stay was justified, as Swik was very fairly treated within the Land Commission, being allowed to retain his six weeks annual leave, plus a certain amount of sick leave, to which he had been entitled under the British regime. He had some disappointments about promotion, but finally was appointed Intelligence and Statistical Officer, adding with a twinkle in his eye that he liked to stress the Intelligence!

Swik's mother in Skibbereen was in poor health during the early part of the year and died on 24 May.

Despite Lucy's earlier forebodings, this pregnancy proceeded normally. She gradually withdrew from committee activities and on 22 September 1923 'At 4 a.m. Daisy Lawrenson Kingston was born, with remarkably little fuss or trouble and with a caul!' Lucy was obviously very bound up in domestic duties over the next months, but had help in the form of a charwoman and also a daily maid, and constant babysitting by Sarah Anne.

1924 was a very busy year for Lucy, firstly in caring for the new baby and sorting out feeding problems which arose. Ralph was a little jealous and showed displayed an 'anti-mother' attitude, but this passed. Lucy was also concerned about Swik being over-stressed. With Willie still abroad, much of the Kingston family affairs such as income tax were left to Swik, and he was very hard-pressed in his office and seeking better conditions.

In June, Lucy, Swik and the children went down to visit Swik's sisters Rachel and Wilhelmina, then living in Park Cottage, Union Hall, with a view across to the lovely village of Glandore. Lucy described it as a 'lovely spot that beggars description. All enjoy a quiet and rather walkative and very talkative holiday.'

On her return to Dublin Lucy advertised for a 'mother's help' as Mrs Langan, who had been a most reliable domestic help for some years, had given notice. Lucy employed a Miss R. who seemed 'very decent and jolly.' As they had planned a second holiday, this time to Switzerland and Paris with Rose Jacob, they arranged that Miss R. would move over to 'Mirtna' with the children and care for them there with Sarah Anne. This was a wise decision as Miss R. turned out to be semi-insane, religiously and otherwise. Lucy's entry, on returning from a most enjoyable foreign trip, was 'Back to vicissitudes at home which seem to have no end. Find Miss R. has made serious mischief between self and Winnie and also Mammie involved, through her eternal religious discussions. Daisy well but unclean. The R. gets madder and more loquacious each day—I long for the end. Friday night she contemplates ending her life in the canal and tries to start out about 1 a.m. to do so. Next night she declares she has poison in her room. I send her out to Mirtna while I search everything for it but find it nowhere. Sunday is a fairly quiet day, but at night she keeps requesting prayers up to 2 a.m. On Monday I try to advise her, it being the last day, and get torrents of abuse as a result. She then starts howling like a dog. I am afraid to go out as intended as it would be dangerous to leave her in

this state, so stay in. Mammie and Dora get frightened and telephone for Swik who comes home to lunch. I suggest his going down to her cousins in North Strand which he does and the young girl comes up about 4 p.m. for her. After waiting some time and giving more cheek and generally behaving like a madwoman, she goes off.' The family was persecuted by Miss R. writing and calling for some time. Fortunately, they were able to get a new and satisfactory help, Alice Byrne.

This experience with Miss R., who was some form of evangelical Protestant (but distressingly unbalanced), made Lucy resume her usual practice of employing Catholic maids or mother's helps. Several of these later maids came from County Leitrim, which was a particularly depressed area. They arrived with very little idea of housework or cooking, Lucy gave them pretty rudimentary training, and they would then leave for work in England, where they could earn higher wages.

Ralph was then diagnosed as having asthma and they were very anxious about him. It was suggested to them that a move to the milder south side of Dublin might help, so they commenced house hunting, aided by Willie Kingston. He had returned from South Africa for the second time and taken a position in a Dublin firm of solicitors. Swik took a week's sick leave as he had a lingering cold and he and Ralph spent the time in Dalkey where Lucy and Elizabeth visited them. On Swik's return to Crescent Villas with Ralph, Lucy wrote: 'My grass widowhood, the fourth in a year, is over and I am not sorry as the burden of loneliness was very little alleviated and seemed a very long time, so much so that I begin to have a sympathy with widows, with wives of indentured labourers etc. Finish essay on psychology. Buttimer here in evening as we are having the fatted calf. Tell him of desire to move out of Dublin and he instantly says that he would then throw up his lodgings at Clonliffe Road and go to Howth, as we and our appreciation of the records is what keeps him here.'

Ralph had fresh attacks of asthma, Daisy developed pneumonia and Lucy got a bout of influenza, so the end of the year was a difficult time. They had many disappointments in their househunting around the Dalkey area. They were worried about Liam's financial state and his talk of emigration and then came the really bad news about Swik's health. He had a polypus removed from his ear, but had recurring and very painful ear trouble and had finally to face a mastoid operation to save his life, as the inflamation was eating in to the brain. A date was fixed in early January. Lucy wrote around this time: 'Propose rewriting Book of Job with ourselves (and 'Mirtna') as principals.'

CHAPTER THIRTEEN
1925–1926

Swik had his operation at the Richmond Hospital on 7 January 1925 fully realising the risks involved and preparing himself for the worst. The decayed bone collapsed inwards at the first stroke of the operation and injured the facial nerve, with the result that the right side of his face was paralysed and badly deformed. When he realized this and felt the nauseating after-effects of the ether, and the pain and nerve shock, weakness and depression, he wondered if life was such a good thing after all! However, he made a good recovery. He had to have daily electric massage for his face and found this dreadfully painful, but the paralysis gradually eased, though his face was slightly distorted for the rest of his life. Just after the operation Lucy informed him that they had been offered a five-year lease of 34 Ulverton Road, Dalkey, one of the houses they had inspected, and they closed with the offer and at once advertised 26 Crescent Villas for sale. It fetched £875.

They moved to Dalkey on 6 February taking Willie as a lodger. Lucy noted: 'We get shipshape in a few days and find shop people very obliging and businesslike. Maid Alice who came with us is restive and lonely and talks of not liking Dalkey!' 34 Ulverton Road was a three-storeyed redbrick terrace house on the tramline approaching Dalkey village with a small garden in front and a long walled garden behind. The frequent tram service to the centre of Dublin enabled Lucy to continue her committee and other interests. On 12 February she noted: 'Divorce laws debate in the Dail—very unsatisfactory. No divorce (*a vinculo matrimonia*) but judicial separation without remarriage possible. Divorce possible only if husband changes domicile—not possible at all therefore to the wife.'

By 15 February Buttimer had visited them with definite notions about joining the menage. He asked for all the details about the basement room, but wanted to have two rooms, not one as they had thought. Lucy commented: 'I have cough but get it over in two days as against three months at home' (meaning Glasnevin). In April Buttimer suddenly descended and asked to be given two rooms. He had already given notice to his landlady in any case! They agreed to take him and he arrived in a cab with fourteen packets of gramophone records. Lucy found his advent made very little more work and was a great success 'as he is the first to realise'.

Just after this they received a letter from Swik's sisters suggesting that as Willie was already in Dublin, they should come up and rent half of Ulverton Road house from Lucy and Swik and all live together there! Lucy was very glad to have Buttimer as the reason for not acceding to this request, as Rachel and Wilhelmina were extremely talkative and had never before (and never would) live anywhere but in the environs of Skibbereen. The attraction of the Kingston household continued, however, as Lucy's family sold 'Mirtna' and took a flat in Dun Laoghaire in order to keep in touch more easily. Because Willie Kingston was now living with them as well as Buttimer, when Buttimer went to Switzerland for a holiday, Lucy commented: 'I am now reduced to two husbands'—her ménage probably being viewed as irregular by her neighbours.

Then came the painful entry: '11 May —a bad day. We go to see the last of Liam at the flat. Mammie and Dora in bad state. Feel can do little to help them. Liam is bearing up well but looks broken-hearted. Whole thing frightfully sad—how will it end?' This refers to the emigration of Liam to USA in the hope that he could make a livelihood there before being joined by Dora and Elizabeth.

Lucy was urged by the Women's International League committee to attend a conference in Innsbruck so she made arrangements to go. A distant cousin, Alice

Woodroofe, agreed to come and take charge of the children and run the house in her absence. She departed on 7 July: 'Go off on boat feeling strange, and weird and lonely.' Lucy enjoyed the conference and also meeting people in London on her return journey, but felt very tired for a few days after her homecoming.

At the AGM of the Irish Section of WILPF in October, Lucy and Rose Jacob were elected joint honorary secretaries and they worked well together. Lucy was sensitive to criticism and there was occasional tension between Miss Louie Bennett and herself. While Lucy admired Miss Bennett's abilities, she resented her authoritarian manner and found her difficult to work with as a result.

Having been proposed earlier in the year as a committee member of the Irish Women Citizens and Local Government Association (which had inherited some of the aims of the earlier Irish Women's Suffrage and Local Government Association), Lucy noted in November that the business before the committee was the government's new attempt to exclude women from the civil service in the Civil Service Reform Bill. Lobbying was immediately undertaken by the Women Citizens Association.

Lucy and Rose had a considerable amount of work as joint secretaries of WILPF as Ireland was chosen by headquarters in Geneva to be the venue for the fifth international congress. The Irish section committee members were then Miss Louie Bennett, Miss Helen Chenevix, Mrs M'Clintock Dix, Mrs Marie Johnson (Hon Treasurer), Miss Molyneux, Miss Mills, Mrs J. Richardson, Mrs M. Stephens and Miss G. Webb. Lucy's letter to Geneva on 1 January 1926 shows the careful planning of the venue: 'I write to tell you that we have got some information that there is a possibility of our getting the National University or the Mansion House free of charge for the congress. We cannot build too much upon this hope as yet; but it would seem that it is at last breaking in upon our government that we shall be doing our city a service in bringing these visitors to Ireland and that it is up to the government to give them some municipal recognition. At the same time we are careful (and must continue to be so) not to put our branch too greatly under the government 'wing' or under too great obligation to them. This would incriminate our league with a certain section of the public. I shall write you again when we know definitely about this matter—what a relief to our treasurer if we could get free buildings for our meetings!' They did eventually get the university buildings in Earlsfort Terrace free and Lucy encouraged the international secretary to write a letter of thanks to the university President, Dr Coffey.

From October 1923 there had been occasional mention of Frederick Budds, a colleague of Winnie's in the Education Office, as being a suitor of Winnie, but they did not become formally engaged as they frequently quarrelled. By 1926 they were house-hunting and were sometimes joined by Lucy who was interested in their eventual purchase of 'Riva' on Coliemore Road, despite constant rows. In April Winnie supplied more drama as Lucy reported: 'Winnie and Budds have big blow-up— this in spite of all the trousseau having been bought, house etc. etc. Consternation. Mammie writes to Budds.' Here was poor Sarah Anne stepping into the breach once more! She wanted Winnie to break it off, but feared she would refuse to do so, so she wrote to Fred to clarify the position about the house.

On 26 April Lucy commented: 'Wedding presents coming pouring in satisfactorily to W. and Budds. All is now peace there', and on May 6: 'The wedding. I bridesmaid and Swik "gave her away". Usual family altercation about the service beforehand and usual result— bowing of heads to convention.' This was the old sore of the 'obey' vow coming up again, but Winnie would not have had as strong support in trying to evade it as had

Lucy from Swik in 1914. Fred Budds was a much more conventional man and a staunch member of the Church of Ireland, later a member of the vestry of Dalkey parish.

This excitement was hardly over before another very important decision faced Lucy and Swik. They had been house-hunting themselves, partly because 34 Ulverton Road was held only on a five-year lease and also because of its distance from the sea. The trek from the far side of Dalkey village, up Sorrento Road and along Vico Road to flights of slippery steps down to the White Rock Strand meant several miles to traverse with all the bathing equipment, and a go-car (as buggies were then termed) to push along also. This journey was very frequently undertaken as Lucy loved swimming and also believed it would help to strengthen Ralph and reduce the number of his asthma attacks.

They heard that 8 Sorrento Terrace was for sale and on 11 May Lucy's entry was: 'Sorrento Terrace house en tapis for us!! S. and I and Buttimer go forth to see it and get in through a window. Am so tired that I feel appalled at size and vastness and thought of our moving. S. to my surprise doesn't seem to share this feeling and we postpone consideration till after congress. Buttimer very keen— much talk and discussion.' Two days later 'the Sorrento Terrace house looms on us and causes excitement.' On 29 May Dick Mansfield, who had recently become engaged, offered to take a flat in the house without his fiancée even seeing it. This decided them to take the house and Swik proceeded with the arrangements as Lucy was so deeply involved in the preparations for the congress in July.

In June Lucy had to speak at a Rotary Club luncheon on behalf of WILPF. She recorded: 'Great attendance, over 100 I think, and plenty of smoke...Get on all right and appear to amuse them by my jokes. Mrs Dix speaks for about fifteen minutes on cases in which war has been prevented. Good press and photos!!' A week later she added: 'Pleasant plaudits from an unknown Rotarian via Haydock (colleague of Swik's) give me temporary head-swellings.'

On 15 June Swik met Gertrud Baer (delegate to the WILPF Congress) at Dun Laoghaire pier and she stayed with them for a few days: 'a charming and interesting personality.' The congress took place from 9–16 July with 150 women representing twenty-two countries on the theme 'Next Steps Towards Peace.' Lucy was so involved that her diary comment was brief: 'The executive committee starts on 7 July and the rest needs no chronicle so will make none. Outstanding people (to me) are Jane Addams, Gertrud Baer and Illova (best spirits) while I am glad to have made acquaintance of Mrs Hayman and Ruth Fry and Dr Hilda Clark (all Quakers).' There was a large garden party hosted by the Governor-General in Phoenix Park and considerable press coverage. Lucy was able to spend two nights with Rose Jacob to enable her to stay for the later evening events and a ceilidh. Dora took on Lucy's housekeeping for nearly a fortnight and Lucy also had support from her next-door neighbour Olive Goodbody who took Daisy every morning.

The congress safely and successfully over, 23 July was moving day. It was a pouring day with thunder. Work continued until 9 p.m., and then the storm kept them awake. Kathleen Collins, Lucy's help, was in very bad form. There followed three days of strenuous toil and deep depression on Lucy's part. This is hardly surprising, in view of her overworked condition for the past six months, but it seemed to stir up her grief over Elsie's death. She copied into her diary a poem entitled 'Burial' by Luba Kaftannikoff, which must have afforded her a way of coming to terms with her continuing sense of loss. The poem compares the mourner's 'safe hearthstone, lit by lamp and flame, where children of love and promise, bring me their ceaseless claim' with the lonely grave of an inspiring companion. Again comes the refrain about children calling her back from her sorrow and her feeling that 'mourning would mar and maim'.

The poet was a half-Russian, half-Irish woman living and writing in Dublin at that period. She later developed a very great interest in the Burren in County Clare and went to live there. She died in the 1960s.

CHAPTER FOURTEEN
1926–1928

A new life now opened up for Swik, Lucy and the children, yet the old pattern was repeated for Lucy, with her mother and sisters living down the hill less than five minutes' walk away.

L. A. G. Strong's description of 8 Sorrento Terrace in *The Garden* is in no way an exaggeration:

> The view it faced so blankly was one of the most beautiful in the world. High on the promontory of Dalkey Sound, with the Island on its left, the house looked full across the Bay of Killiney to the Wicklow Mountains. The pure line, the nobility, the ease and grace of that long curving prospect has never been captured in paint or words ...Those whose houses look out upon it see it every morning anew. Those who see it for the first time are apt to be silent. It is liberal, free, and unstaged: no point monopolises it...

Strong was related to the Barton family from whom Swik and Lucy had bought the house. Mrs Florence Barton and her daughter Nora had suffered the loss of son and brother Vivian Barton, who had been killed in France in 1917. In a basement room were still posters showing his craze for motor cycles, and when a top stair creaked at night (quite customary in old houses when cooling) we used to remark fondly 'Ah, Barton's ghost.'

Dalkey was then a pleasant small village and a quiet residential area. The terrace was inhabited by a mixture of teachers, civil servants, housewives, one solicitor and one professor and, next-door in Number 7, a retired civil engineer. There was no hint of the present-day high executive image and life was very simple. Rooms were large and hard to heat, there was only gas lighting and cooking and the Kingstons had no transport other than bicycles. Being the end of the Terrace, Number 8 was larger, as the architect had rounded off the building in 1874 with an extra large room on each floor, and inserted four large windows in the curved end of each. There was also a larger garden, with three lawns connected by steep slopes (a joy for children, but difficult to maintain). There was also a large greenhouse with flourishing vines and heliotrope. All this for a payment of £400 for the lease, plus £20 commission!

One thing the terrace residents shared were storms, but these were most severe at our south-west end and Lucy never became acclimatised to the noise and attendant worry as slates were repeatedly torn off. Once a whole pane of glass was sucked out and hurled in the path of a litigious tenant of the flat! Swik now spent much of his leisure crawling round on the roof, partly for reasons of economy but also because, with his very light and agile frame, he felt better fitted for the task than sturdier workmen. It is perhaps significant that his diaries cease in 1926 as house repairs thereafter took so much of his time and attention.

Another more pleasant aspect shared with the other residents (with the exception of Number 1 which had its own shoreline right round Sorrento Point) was the rocky bathing place at the foot of shared cliffs. Gorse-perfumed paths led down from each back-garden door to a boat-slip and at high tide there was over eight feet depth of clean, cold water.

The house, as originally designed, had a large basement kitchen with small adjoining bedrooms for staff, plus one large sitting room. This floor had a separate hall-door approached by descending steps and a pathway to the side of the house so, by partitioning off the stairs, it was made into a self-contained flat for Dick and Bella Mansfield who moved in almost immediately. It took

Lucy some time to get to know Bella but Dick was, of course, a long-established friend, as well as being Swik's step-nephew. The Mansfields paid £54 per annum for this spacious flat.

A great feature of the Kingstons' part of the house was that one of the drawing-room windows could be raised high enough to allow access to a wooden stairs down to a wide balcony. From this a small circular iron staircase led down to the garden level. Owing to their being built on a cliff (originally an old lead mine), the eight houses were three-storeys in front, facing the road, but four-storeys at the rear. This rear basement level included a wine-cellar, coal-cellar and various storerooms and the one sunny room which had been Vivian Barton's den in number 8.

Buttimer had a large room with three windows facing the road. This housed his gramophone with its huge horn, and his large collection of records. He never closed shutters or pulled curtains, so speculation abounded in Dalkey as to what this bald-headed figure was doing sitting so still, illuminated only by the pink glow of a paraffin stove!

Lucy had many visitors during the next few months and loved to show the house. However, she was still very busy with her committee work and was appointed by WILPF to take part in a debate with Blackrock Debating Society. This was greatly on her mind. Her account of it on 4 December reads: 'Helen Chenevix and self, palpitating, go to Technical School in Blackrock and hold forth. Successful and interesting meeting and have not to read my speech except from notes. She does likewise. McKenna, Cotton and Seán Ó hUadaigh speak, last is chairman. O'Keeffe sees us back to train—all very nice and collection of pacifist speeches encouraging! I am 'speaker of distinction and evident ability, well used to debate', forsooth, which causes me to sing a bawdy song internally.'

Their first Sorrento Christmas Day was described thus:

'All Rivas and Buttimer come to dinner—we sing carols outside Dick's door inspired by thin sherry and much diluted port. All stay to tea also and young Piatt joins us.' Her Boyd cousins had provided a turkey and the food for so many was stored and cooked in the very basic little kitchen by her resident help, Kathleen Collins.

The New Year of 1927 started well for Lucy and family with numerous parties. These were at various friends' houses and also at Friends (Quakers) as Lucy was attending the local Meeting at Monkstown. On 6 January Lucy noted that she and Swik had attended a memorable performance of *Emperor Jones* at the Abbey. At the end of January there was a bad storm, shrieks of wind, and eighteen slates off.

In February Lucy brought up the subject of birth control at the Irish Women Citizens Association committee (successor to the IWSLGA previously mentioned), as there was an account of the scandalous Commission on Evil Literature in the *Irish Times*. Lucy noted in her diary about this time the following quotation from Sir Arthur Newsholme:

> Human welfare is now menaced by human fecundity…By medicine and by hygiene Nature's destructive forces have been conquered. But the victory will be disastrous to human welfare unless a desire for many children, which is natural and until recently was laudable, is held in check.

March was a worrying month for Lucy and she had to abandon many committees. Ralph had a bad asthma attack following a heavy cold and next Daisy, who had been having symptoms of gastritis with a temperature of 104, took a new turn. Instead of desperate crossness and hunger (having been on slops for over a week) she was now calm, tired and quiescent, not asking for food or anything else. Old Dr Wright and his son were attending but did not throw much light. It was feared that there was kidney trouble and chill. On 28 March Lucy wrote: 'A bad day. S. brings home news that Edward Harvey has consulted five doctors over Daisy's state and all, including Dr Joseph Wigham, agree there is danger of TB of stomach. Plunged into anxiety surpassing all that went before. Yet she shows signs of improving.' Next day: 'Swik goes to have interview with Dr Wigham this evening who reassures us and has noticed no signs of TB, though has had hundreds of cases of it in children. Greatly bucked.'

In the midst of all this there had been trouble in 'Riva' so Dora and Elizabeth had moved out and spent three weeks with Lucy to let things simmer down!

One of the pleasures of living in Sorrento for Lucy was being able to hold whist and bridge drives, as six tables could be managed in the drawing room. She also enjoyed giving combined children's parties (for Ralph's, Elizabeth's and Daisy's friends) at which the children had plenty of room to play in garden and 'on the rocks' as beyond the garden gate was called.

On 10 July 1927 Lucy wrote: 'We are staggered to hear news of shooting of Kevin O'Higgins at Cross Avenue, Booterstown, outside San Souci. Milk boy brings tale.' This was the assassination of the man who was Vice-President, Minister for Justice and Minister for External Affairs in the new Cosgrave administration. There was never any evidence of Republican complicity in his death and de Valera was unequivocal in his condemnation of the murder, but very stringent public safety laws were enforced as a result.

In August Lucy had an opportunity to join the Culwick Choir when they went to compete in the Eisteddfod (Welsh festival of music, drama and song) in Llandudno. 'We get on to perfection, winning £150 for mixed choir and £30 for Ladies. Holyhead press and public go wild. Congrats. abound. Greatly impressed with Eisteddfod and all its ways.'

In October Lucy noted: 'Go by invitation to Mrs

Bewley's where first have coffee and then hear Mrs
Corbett Ashby (most eloquent, nicest and most optimistic
speaker I have heard for a long time). She holds forth for a
long time (over an hour) and gives account of League of
Nations and women's laws all over the world. Rooms
crammed.' Mrs Corbett Ashby was President of the
United Kingdom branch of the International Alliance of
Women.

On 14 October Lucy attended the Annual General
Meeting of WILPF. 'Mrs Sheehy Skeffington brings in
resolution on women in public life, Rose Jacob resigns but
takes good part in debate. I speak on birth control (!!) or
rather on world population and to my surprise get almost
unanimity in resolution to take part in future conferences
and appoint commission on subject. I get letter from Dr
Marie Stopes!' In September Lucy had written an article
on the Irish elections for *Women's Leader*, with specific
reference to birth control and the report of the
Commission on Evil Literature and Dr Stopes had seen the
article.

On 28 October Lucy went to Dublin to attend a lecture
but there was such a storm that few came. 'Coming home
is a great experience— train stopped by felled tree. Engine
driver injured. Telephone wires crash down on us, also
pole. We get out at Merrion Gates where a chimney falls.
Get on to tram and at Ulverton Road a wrecked garage
roof is blown around. Surprising to say the Terrace is calm
but we have suffered loss and shock—rain pouring in all
back windows. Five slates off and coping damaged.
Nearly every house in Dalkey has slates off. Big storm.
Seventy-three fishermen lost off west coast.'

At the end of January, 1928 Lucy noted: 'I spend most
of day in bed tended by my good mother. Read
meanwhile H. G. Wells and Walter de la Mare. Do not feel
very much up to mark—have no doubts of events now but
wary of miscarriage—the usual fear.' Having earlier been
quite sure that their family of one boy and one girl was

sufficient, Lucy had begun to wish for another child and had persuaded the cautious Swik that they should at least try again.

On 11 February her entry was: 'Go in by appointment to meet Mrs Stephens and Mrs Sheehy Skeffington and see J. Montgomery the Film Censor and have a most interesting interview, helped out by his loquacity and niceness and by Mrs S.S's wit. We are shown the cinema room, and many reports read from his notes. Upshot: We are to try to get a joint deputation to ask for insertion of a clause including war films in the act.' Censorship of films was being set up and the Irish Section of WILPF were anxious that war films should be banned. Lucy also got Quaker support for this.

For the next few months Lucy's diary continues to note various committees and social occasions such as whist drives at neighbours' houses. In mid-April 1928 Lucy took the chair at a meeting where Helen Chenevix and Louie Bennett gave interesting speeches re Geneva and disarmament and a good deal of discussion followed.

Then on 24 April she noted: 'Mammie and I go to Dun Laoghaire in morning. Notice she is a little slower on her feet these days, and one morning this week she gets slight weakness when coming up here. She goes into Dublin on Wednesday and Saturday and into Dalkey twice this week.' On 28 March: 'Mammie goes to enquire for the new Seale baby—back tired about 8 o'clock.' Her next entry is heavily underlined: 'Sunday 29 A new life for us all from this morning for Mammie passes away at 4 o'clock and a link that never can be mended is broken. I am the first to be called up at 3.45 by Fred as I sleep in the front and happen to be awake at the time. Think it is nothing but bilious attack and hesitate to waken the others. After about twenty minutes he comes back again. I rouse Dora and Swik and we all go down to 'Riva'. Dr Wright has been there but too late. Over-exertion and heart failure are the cause of her sudden death. After two awful days that seem endless the funeral takes place a 3 o'clock at St. George's Burial Ground, Tom Seale reading the service.'

Lucy then accompanied her Aunt Janie back to Ballinglen and visited various relatives in the area, telling them about Sarah Anne's death. She returned to Dalkey on 17 May and Winnie and Fred came up to hear how she had got on. Two days later, Lucy noted: 'Our weekly calamity—Winnie gets miscarriage last night and is ordered in to Rotunda Hospital.'

Then Lucy noted: 'Swik's lines to S.A.L. are typed by me and sent to various people, including Mrs Jones who has been so very much more like a relation than the relations themselves. I read and am fascinated with an old diary of Mammie's beginning before Ralphie's death, dealing with those two harrowing items (and many other harrowing ones too) and ending up at 'Marlton' and me a year old.' Lucy also noted that Daisy was 'wearing at present little Ralphie's navy-blue coat frock made by Mammie for him about forty-five years ago!' These old diaries are where we first met Sarah Anne.

CHAPTER FIFTEEN
1928–1929

From now on for many years Lucy had fairly frequent evenings at home playing piano duets with Tom Harrison (Liam's brother) and Victor Davies, a friend from nearby Glenageary. This encouraged Lucy to keep up regular practice and, of course, there were many musical recitals on Buttimer's gramophone. Kathleen Collins left but Lucy found an excellent replacement in Lil Kinsella and there were many references to how satisfactory and pleasant she found her. Daisy developed acute ear trouble and had to be brought to Pembroke Private Hospital where her tonsils and adenoids were removed. Lucy stayed with her and enjoyed the brief break, reading a life of Mary Shelley and concocting a poem 'Night in the Hospital' during a rather disturbed night. Early in July there was a party for thirty-one children and nine adults. A very cold storm arose so tea was served in the greenhouse.

Later in July there was a rare mention of Winnie's domestic scene: 'Winnie giving in all along the line as regards her wishes and rights, and now thinks of postponing visit to USA for five or six years (!) on the advice of the partner. Greatly puzzled as to what has become of her personality, not to say irritated, and of course anything I say on the matter is put down to my being over-zealous on the woman question.' Winnie had obviously changed considerably since her suffragette days.

Then came the great wrench of parting with Dora and Elizabeth. 'Dora starts this morning, I going to see them off at "Riva" and Ralph and Swik going to Kingstown, while Winnie goes to Manchester and stays a few days at Colwyn Bay. I come back and write to Aunt Janie to relieve my feelings and her loneliness. Ralph much cut up at losing Elizabeth. He and Daisy at daggers drawn these days, which distresses us. I knit furiously, an anodyne.'

Dora and Elizabeth were reunited with Liam but Dora had much adjusting to do and homesickness and depression to overcome. She wrote long descriptive letters to both sisters and they replied, Winnie especially telling every detail of the home scene to keep Dora in touch.

The arts of illumination and heraldry were at that time almost wholly unknown in that part of the United States, so Dora had first to introduce them to interested people in the north-west by means of innumerable lectures. This was a new skill which Dora found a challenge and finally came to enjoy. She wrote entertainingly to her sisters on the sartorial variations she performed on the black evening dress she had brought over with her. Throughout her years of public life she managed to dress for formal occasions with flair and inventiveness, to compensate for having very little spare cash for clothes.

In September Lucy was busy writing to various Quaker and political figures to try to get amendments to the Evil Literature Censorship Bill which 'we have got and perused and which is exciting comment and correspondence in press. An insidious move against birth control.'

Lucy's 'coming event' (as she always referred to her confinement) was long delayed and she and the midwife took long walks around Dalkey and Killiney hoping to encourage it. Then on 13 October Elsa Lawrenson Kingston was born. Daisy had been sent away to stay with friends but Ralph was at home, and Lucy commented that he was greatly improved by the event and entertained her during convalescence. Lucy had a great number of visitors whom she listed with evident pleasure, and remarked on the great enthusiasm with which Elsa was greeted in the house.

On 24 November she noted: 'Frightful gales all over the world—we escape with one or two slates this time, much to our relief, but widespread damage done elsewhere and the *Daily Mail* has an article on the gale mystery.' She also added 'Censorship Bill furore. Mrs Sheehy Skeffington has been in London speaking on Censorship Bill—as everyone is at present.' Rose Jacob visited Lucy in great form and eloquent on the question of capital punishment and jury system.

Lucy commented sadly: 'Seem to miss Mammie greatly these times—thinking a good deal of her and of Elsie lately and of how few there are left who know our family traditions'—which comment is surprising, as Lucy always seemed to scoff at tradition.

Swik had to take sick leave in December as he had gallstone trouble but recovered without an operation. Lucy ended the year with: 'We grow patient and angelic day by day through dint of the afflictions with which we have been visited in 1928: nonetheless we hope for better luck in 1929.

The Censorship Bill was still news and Swik and Lucy attended a debate on it in the Rotunda Rooms in January 1929: 'John Brennan [the journalist Sidney Gifford Czira] and R. M. Fox v. Fianna Fail TDs Brady and Little. Very interesting. John Brennan moves Swik to enthusiasm. Rose Jacob plunges into birth control subject bravely. Most entertaining.'

There was an influenza epidemic and, after nursing Lil, her help, for two days Lucy got a temperature of 103 degrees. Fortunately, the midwife was able to come for a few days and Lucy managed to keep up the breastfeeding of Elsa. She recovered quickly but was dep;ressed for some time. She derived great pleasure from Elsa. Comments such as 'Babe teething hard but usually very good and jolly—looks around with kind wise eyes full of humour' and 'One fair fascinator' crop up. On 15 July Winnie had a son, Robert William Salter Budds, and all went well. Lucy saw the healthy infant next day.

Lucy and Swik set off for a walking holiday in Connemara: 'Very good holiday and costs only £5 and some footsoreness. Greatly struck by Connemara's desolation and poverty and think we know all about it now.'

On 31 August Lucy's entry was: 'Electrified to hear of Miss Culwick's death. Quite bowled over by the news. Go to poor Miss Culwick's funeral at Leeson Park Church. Coffin left outside: Memorial Service (all choral) and no funeral marches, thank goodness. "Crossing the Bar" and "Nunc Dimittis" etc. sung by St Patrick's men and her own men (about eight of same). Very nice service and great crowds and newspaper recognition. Mrs Stanford tells me the cause of her death—clot of blood, after a successful operation. This is a chapter closed—our connection since 1913 with choir finally broken.'

On 11 October Lucy wrote: 'Go to WILPF committee and am much troubled over their fortunes (or lack of same). Mrs S.S. in the Chair and makes complaint afterwards (for me to pass on to Women Citizens) about treatment of emigrants at hands of American doctor and officials at passport office.'

The end of October was their fifteenth wedding anniversary and Swik's celebration of those fulfilling years was to present Lucy with the following poem:

My Ideal Wife

She is beautiful, clever, charming, she is loyal, kind,
  sincere,
Her soul is tuned to the highest, her intellect crystal
  clear.
She is dignified, graceful, modest, she is witty,
  humourous, wise.
Health shines from her clear complexion and her
  sparkling grey-blue eyes.
Sweet music springs from her fingers, sweet notes
  from her tuneful voice,
And the light of her gracious presence makes her
  hearth and home rejoice.

The pen of the ready writer, the grace of the poet's
  line

Are hers—yet with steadfast duty she never will
  proud decline
The thrifty care of her household, of her bonny
  children three
The endless tasks of the woman who a poor man's
  wife will be.
Yet ever she works to further the sacred pursuit of
  peace
And snatches from duty's rigour but brief and scant
  release.
But then with a child's abandon she can freely
  unbend in play
Or tramp with a stick and knapsack the whole of a
  summer's day.
A man's unique companion, a man's true tender
  wife—
Queen of my heart I hold her, the dearest thing in
  life.

                                        SWK October 1929.

They also celebrated by seeing Mrs Patrick Campbell play
in *Ghosts* in December. Lucy had been reading her *Life and
Letters* which gave this occasion added interest.

CHAPTER SIXTEEN
1930–1933

In February 1930 Lucy was appointed delegate to the next WILPF congress which was to take place in April in Geneva. However, during March and early April Daisy developed acute ear trouble which a locum attempted to treat in the absence of their usual specialist. Lucy had therefore to cancel her plans and Louie Bennett attended the congress.

By 28 April Daisy was in such pain that Lucy brought her in to the specialist, who had just returned. After one look at the child's ear he ordered her straight into the Richmond Hospital and performed an emergency mastoid operation that night. In view of Swik's awful experience after his operation, this was a profoundly worrying time for the parents, but the surgery was entirely successful and Daisy returned home after about three weeks.

In June Lucy attended a conference at the Irish Women Workers' Union: 'Affiliation Orders Bill and other matters re the position of unmarried mothers: problem of prostitution etc. Very interesting. Father Devane is the moving spirit in these things. Dean Kennedy also speaks: Senator Wyse Power in Chair.' This union had been founded in 1911 with Delia Larkin as secretary but in 1916 Louie Bennett had taken over the leadership, always ably assisted by Helen Chenevix.

Lucy's next excitement was the visit to Dublin of Professor Chakravarty. The Irish Section of WILPF had been trying to arrange a visit from the Indian poet Rabindranath Tagore, who was spending some time at the Quaker College in Birmingham. He was not able to come but sent his secretary instead. There was increasing interest in Indian affairs at this time and Lucy had earlier noted: 'We talk of Gandhi whose salt-gathering campaign is the talk of the world.'

On 27 July: 'The Indian Professor Chakravarty arrives by evening boat—I go out after committee by myself and meet him—a little frail young-looking man.' Next day: 'Take chair at Engineer's Hall for Chakravarty—audience only medium size but a good deal to account for this. A paper read which is rather above our heads, but questions bring forth a most exhaustive amount of information and we are all delighted (especially the more spiritually minded of us) with the character and charm of our speaker.' Two days later: 'Repair to the reception at Trinity Hall, very enjoyable and a good crowd. Chakravarty shows signs of being tired but is very interesting on Bengal women's movement.' Next day: 'Meeting at Wynn's Hotel, very well filled. Mrs Sheehy Skeffington takes the chair with her usual skill (this sounds like journalese!). The non-violent movement of India—beginning with religious basis and going on to Gandhi's speeches and proclamations. Answers are very good—but he is dropping with tiredness.' On 3 July Lucy wrote: 'Am psychically as well as physically disturbed these nights and cannot sleep. Feel nervous about sale as weather is very uncertain. Today is a fright—thunderstorms and torrential rain. We assemble for the sale indoors at 3.30. A great crowd turn up considering and thirteen come from Dalkey. He speaks on subject of Santiniketan Bengal and we have tea at 5.30 and then the sale and step-dance from Rose etc. He speaks of having not known a soul in Ireland a week ago and now: 'I haf so many friends—it is wonderful!' Yes, indeed, charming Chakravarty! I think it is we whom you have left with an inferiority complex now!'.

Lucy was deeply impressed by this visitor and immediately began reading *Glimpses of Bengal* by Tagore. Later in the year she read *Letters to a Friend* by Tagore (these being to C. F. Andrews,) and the following year *The Indian Outlook* by W. D. S. Holland, *My Own Story* by Mahatma Gandhi, edited by C. F. Andrews, and *The*

Religion of Man by Tagore.

On 18 August Lucy noted: 'Charles Jacob comes tonight bringing raspberries and the news that Swik is accepted into Society of Friends!' This was just confirmation that his application had gone through. Charles Jacob lived in Dalkey and Lucy frequently mentioned that he had driven her back from evening meetings. From the time they moved to Sorrento Road, and for many years until they acquired their own transport, they had been conveyed to and from Monkstown Meeting by the Pearson family who lived in Sorrento Road. The Pearsons were a naturally punctual family and the Kingstons (especially Lucy) tended to cut timing very fine, so the unfailing courtesy, patience and friendship of the Pearsons was greatly appreciated.

Lucy was always anxious to share her enthusiasms and felt the Quakers should take more interest in the developments in India. She told them of the forthcoming conference in Worcester arranged by the Fellowship of Reconciliation and, after much discussion, they appointed an elderly Friend to attend. Lucy herself was also to represent them, but she and Rose Jacob were attending as FOR representatives also.

In early September she and Rose Jacob attended this conference held in Arley Castle. 'To our great delight Chakravarty appeared on the castle steps as we return from a walk on Sunday and behold, his wife in Indian dress, a beauteous vision. We see her again the following Wednesday with Rabindranath Tagore's daughter-in-law when they come to take Chakravarty away on the first step of his journey to Russia. We have one walk with him and a few short conversational snatches, and he gives two lectures, all on as high a spiritual plane as usual. Hopes to come to Ireland again in New Year before going back to India: and asks us to Birmingham and, of course, talks of 'when you come to India'. Greatly enjoy conference but utterly nauseated towards end by the Englishness of the 'spirituality' and prayer—complain to Rose that it is in danger of doing us spiritual injury to be there—and physical injury to laugh so much in secret ... Rose and I speak (after request)—I on parallels between India and Ireland etc. and she gives WILPF message'.

Later that month Lucy and the other representative reported back to the Quakers, speaking for about twelve minutes: 'All seem very interested and a pin could be heard drop while we speak. No controversy and I am glad to have had opportunity.'

In mid-August Swik took Ralph and Daisy to Ballinglen, returning after a few days. Lucy had had visitors but nevertheless commented: 'Swik returns by 1.17 train to my great relief as yesterday was a (teeming) horror of loneliness.' Lucy, though so independent in her activities, relied greatly on Swik's companionship and shared interests to carry out their joint ideal: 'to serve our generation so far as we have talent and opportunity', to quote from his proposal to her in 1913.

Towards the end of September Lucy and Daisy went for a few days to visit relations in County Carlow. 'Haycocks submerged, rivers flooded, corn ruined and nothing talked of but the prospect of famine. This year worst since Black '47.'

In January 1931 Lucy noted in her diary: 'Long letter from Dora. She is preparing a forty-five minute lecture for 1 February at Arts Club, one of the best Institutions in Seattle. How funny to think that she and I in the same week (two tongue-tied Lawrensons) will be haranguing in two different hemispheres, one on heraldic designs, the other on the designs of armament-makers. Too silly for words.'

Lucy's principal preoccupation during 1931 was disarmament. There was to be a disarmament conference under the auspices of the League of Nations in 1932, and all sections of WILPF were asked to collect signatures in support of total disarmament. Lucy threw herself into this work with sustained energy. First she approached the Quakers and they agreed to circulate all their Meetings countrywide with forms for signature. Lucy enlisted the willing help of Mona, her mother's help, to canvas around their local area. Lucy also took every opportunity to speak publicly in schools, the Church of Ireland Training College and the Irish Women Workers' Union. She had trained herself very early in her public life to speak with only a few notes for reference and she was aware of the advantages of brevity and wit.

A quotation from A. Ponsonby's *Now is the Time* was copied into her diary and she may have used it in some of her speeches: 'I maintain that war achieves no single object of advantage in the high sense to anyone, nor does it attain any of the supposed aims for which it is waged...The sight of the Allied Powers first making a supreme physical effort to destroy and annihilate their foe, and then making a far more prolonged, yet still unsuccessful effort to set that selfsame foe on his feet, in their own interest, is in itself a striking epitome of the inanity of war.'

There was some initial disagreement within the Irish section over this subject and an International Disarmament Declaration Committee was formed with some of the original WILPF members. They wrote to the head office in Geneva to explain the split. By 17 July Lucy had 6000 signatures in her possession, even sending forms to Dora in Seattle for signature. These Dora successfully had completed, writing to someone about 'my young sister Lucy of whom I am inordinately proud'. On 11 July Lucy noted: 'Great Albert Hall peace meeting in London. March of 500,000 women starting from Embankment at 1.30. WILPF is the initiator of all this.'

At the beginning of August Lucy went to a 'No More War' conference in Holland and was particularly interested to see the Peace Palace at The Hague, Leiden University, crèches in Amsterdam and so on.

On 1 September Lucy went to Rose's flat to have tea with her and Owen Sheehy Skeffington 'whom I like well and think very unformidable considering his parents and his attainments'. She and Rose then went to canvass a cinema queue. They toiled away for one and a half hours and did well, getting ninety names on their disarmament petition.

In November the International Disarmament Declaration Committee joined with the League of Nations Society to hold a meeting in Wynn's Hotel. Dr Hilda Clark from England spoke on 'The World Crisis and Disarmament' and Rev Stephen J Brown, SJ took the chair. Lucy was pleased that crowds attended and some offered to take forms for signature. She noted later: 'Write to Dr Clark and send cuttings and thanks—a grown-up personality if ever there was one, and her face alone a sermon'.

There was some hope that Gandhi might visit Dublin after his London visit but on 5 December Lucy noted: 'Everyone anxious about English financial crisis, about Manchurian crisis, about the German crisis, about the Indian crisis—nothing but crises and crises, and rumours and alarms. Where will it all end? Gandhi is now on his way home to India. Will civil disobedience restart now?'

Lucy was amused by a visitor's comment on Swik's appearance 'Now that is a real nice looking man: I don't mean he is so very pretty looking, but he has an affectionate sort of a face!'

In early December Lucy went to Ballinglen with Elsa and commented that Elsa was even quainter than usual while there, and was wearing Ralphie's dress, re-dyed and piped with red, which was now nearly fifty years old and a curiosity. Sarah Anne must have been a very expert needlewoman who used durable materials.

In December WILPF arranged a sale of work—more goods than buyers. Lucy wrote: 'I get my fortune told ("Strong-willed, great strength of purpose, self-reliant to a degree, wide views, strong head, a remarkable judge of character, a successful woman")—'O Lord' was Lucy's response to this!

The beginning of 1932 brought an end to the intensive work on collecting signatures. On 12 January: 'Have last Declaration committee and to my relief they agree to keep on an international committee till end of conference and do any educational work possible. 18000 signatures, I send all this news to three newspapers who publish same meekly. Also send suggestions of names of women to the Ministry of External Affairs who are very polite to us just now—election time being near.'

On 2 February a disarmament intercession service was held at St. Ann's Church in Dawson Street to mark the opening of the League of Nations Conference on Disarmament in Geneva. The progress of the conference was reported back to the Irish section by WILPF members in Geneva.

On 9 February Lucy and Rose went to hear the 'battle of the giants', a debate on trade union matters between Louie Bennett and Miss Sullivan.

Lucy's spritely entry for 19 February shows her preoccupations this year: 'I go to very enjoyable game of bridge. Anxious about Japan and China: anxious about election results: about our committee troubles: about Dora's affairs: about Ralph's health and Elsa's ditto. O whither shall I go then from thy presence, O anxiety-neuroses?—Forget it, forget it!! It was refreshing this morning to get a card from Peet, the new editor of *The Friend*, expressing appreciation of things I had written there last year and asking for more. Must try to think up something bright and sportive that does not reflect my anxiety-neurosis. He puts in my letter about Far Eastern crisis which is an answer to an article defending Japan by a Japanese Quaker.'

The Disarmament Committee acted as hosts to twenty-five War Resisters' International members who came for Whit weekend. Swik and Lucy enjoyed meeting them, a social was held and then they visited Helen Chenevix and Louie Bennett in Killiney. Lucy was particularly interested in hearing talks by a miner, an engine driver and a shop-girl.

In mid-June there was an Eucharistic Congress held in Dublin with tremendous crowds everywhere. 'The Congress is upon us in full force and with a vengeance. I don't think we shall ever forget this week. Tom Harrison prevented from coming for music owing to crowds and we keep out of Dublin for some days. Reception and garden party on Tuesday (20,000 at former) to which Mona goes'. On 21 June: 'Committee postponed owing to congress. Rose here with an imprecation on her lips 'To h—- with the P—-' after missing thirty-five trams in succession! Mona out tonight at state reception (no less) and gets introduced to executive celebrities and invited by Mrs de Valera to tea on Sunday week.' On 26 June: 'Last day of Congress—I hurry back from Friends to let Mona off to have a hectic time in which she is nearly squashed to death and nearly comes home with another person's baby on hands.'

Lucy's reactions must seem somewhat bigoted, but she attempted to rationalise her feelings in some of her following entries: '28 June Hot exhausting day. Have our last committee after which I feel rather discouraged—last week's proceedings may have been thrilling (as Mrs Dix puts it) to Irish Catholics, but nothing exhilarating to the tiny minority who are out for liberty of judgment. Mrs Dix cries off the German trip and also writes me a tearing lecture because I said I longed to leave Ireland for even a week.' Later she replied to Mrs Dix's letter re Ireland and noted that Donn Piatt had a good letter in *Irish Times*. She added sadly: 'Feel aliens in our land these times'. This feeling of alienation and of the triumphalism of the Catholic Church was new to Lucy. She had worked with Catholics before her marriage, and also quite naturally on committees and in her social contacts. However, from the time of the Eucharistic Congress right through the 1940s and 1950s, she was more aware of the tensions that arose on certain issues, especially when anti-communism reached its peak.

At the end of July Lucy, with Ruby and Betty Holt, met fifty-seven War Resisters International members in London and travelled to Cologne for a Conference during which they: 'hear constant wireless election results like the voice of doom'. This is Lucy's first reference to the Nazi movement.

On Lucy's return she saw Eric Metchette for the first time and approved. She knew, of course, about Winnie's decision to adopt a boy so that Robin would have company, as it seemed very unlikely that she would have another child. The adoption was much discussed within the family as Fred was not keen, but Winnie was determined to persevere. Eric was a lovely toddler at that time and grew up to be a most affectionate son for Winnie, but the two boys had little in common, and it was not an easy relationship where Fred was concerned.

Lucy was one of four Quakers to go on a deputation to de Valera on the subject of the League of Nations. 'Rather surprised at the humanity of his presence, but think he is the wrong man for Geneva—evidently only going there to put forward Ireland, not world peace.' This, of course, was her personal opinion, not that of the group.

In September Lucy wrote an article on Germany which was published on the front page of the *Irish Press*. She noted attending a conference of social workers on the problems facing unmarried mothers and the hold-up of the report by government, which she found an interesting meeting.

On 26 October she wrote: 'Swik and I go to see Oscar Wilde's play *An Ideal Husband*—very appropriate in circumstances (eighteen years married).'

In December Lucy attended: 'Our last committee as an International Disarmament Declaration Committee group—some opposition and plenty of discussion, but we agree at last to join Irish League of Nations Society.

Lucy copied into her diary a prayer from Dean Inge which seems characteristic of this stage of her life: 'Lord keep me lean and active of mind and keen of conscience that all my days I may be willing to live dangerously and so live my life in that splendid fullness which is its only justification.'

CHAPTER SEVENTEEN
1933–1939

During the years 1933 to 1939 Lucy became increasingly aware of the growth of Nazism in Germany. She had made attempts earlier on to learn German and resolved to try harder. She was very concerned to hear grave news about Gertrud Baer, Linda Heyman and Dr Augsburg, all WILPF members in Germany, who had become refugees.

All during 1933 the Disarmament Conference had been continuing at the League of Nations and on 21 October Lucy noted: 'The Disarmament Conference on its last legs—sudden withdrawal of Germany from it and from League of Nations and general consternation. It struggles on to try to get some sort of a convention.'

In September 1935 she wrote: 'Watching the League of Nations re Abyssinian crisis. Everyone condemns Italian action and pours curses on Mussolini—but what will they do!'

From 1933 onwards Lucy had maintained her interest in disarmament, despite the disappointment over the failure of the Conference. She spoke to schools and encouraged the formation of junior groups of the League of Nations Societies. She helped to organise monthly League of Nations lunches with interesting speakers. She attended a World Education Conference held in Dublin in July 1933 which included a garden party at the Viceregal Lodge for 2000 guests.

In 1934, through the Quaker Peace Committee, a German Emergency Committee was established by Dublin Quakers and Hilda Webb was appointed convenor. Lucy served on this committee with great interest and enthusiasm, and from then until 1937 helped many Germans either to settle in Ireland or to emigrate.

In 1935 she was appointed to attend the Germany

Yearly Meeting of the Society of Friends and in 1937 she spent a month in Germany. The Quakers were discreetly running a rest home for people who had been temporarily imprisoned in concentration camps for offences against the Nazi regime. Those released were in great need of quiet counselling to restore their nerves and help them to face life again. Lucy wrote no detailed account of her time in Germany, but did try to interest Dublin Quakers and some of her friends on her return.

Lucy was asked by Mrs Salkeld, Miss Ffrench-Mullen and Mrs Reddin to join the Women Writers' Club and she enjoyed their meetings and occasional banquets to honour a writer's new book as, for instance, Rose Jacob's books *The Rise of the United Irishmen* in 1937 and *The Rebel's Wife* in 1958.

Lucy, always ready for new challenges, took up a fresh one in 1934. Since 1930 there had been a friendship between Daisy and Pat Butler, who had lived for a short time with her parents in Sorrento Terrace. When the Butlers moved to Mount Merrion, the friendship continued. Daisy, aged 11, had now outgrown her preparatory school in Dalkey, so when Mrs Butler asked Lucy to take Pat on as pupil/boarder, Lucy consented, and Pat came in January. The venture was not very successful as Pat was delicate and it ended after some months.

In 1933 a German refugee came as a 'house daughter' for a short time. In 1934 Annelies Becker arrived from the Rhineland. She was not a refugee but her mother wanted her to have a freer atmosphere than that prevailing in Germany. The family joke was that she came for three weeks and stayed for nineteen years. She was like an adopted daughter and close friend to Lucy. She trained as a midwife at the Rotunda Hospital and attended private cases throughout the war years.

In 1935 Ralph (nicknamed Clangy) and his close friend Sidney (always known as Dell) Shellard both began work as insurance clerks and continued to play in their own dance band in their free time.

A great family event in September 1935 was the six-month visit of Dora and Elizabeth (then aged fifteen with no trace of American accent). She and Daisy became close friends, arranging theatrical shows to entertain the family at Christmas.

Early in 1936 there was a sudden hurricane, the skylight and two windows were smashed, and 129 slates blown off the roof. There were many storms during the Kingstons' almost twenty years at Sorrento, but this was outstanding. A poem by Ted Hughes (written years later) gives graphic pictures that vividly recall that night to Daisy, Elsa and Elizabeth, and is included here by kind permission:

Wind

This house has been far out at sea all night,
The woods crashing through darkness, the booming
    hills,
Winds stampeding the fields under the window
Floundering black astride and blinding wet

Till day rose; then under an orange sky
The hills had new places, and wind wielded
Blade-light, luminous and emerald.
Flexing like the lens of a mad eye.

At noon I scaled along the house-side as far as
The coal-house door.
I dared once to look up—
Through the brunt wind that dented the balls of my
    eyes
The tent of the hills drummed and strained its
    guyrope,

The fields quivering, the skyline a grimace,
At any second to bang and vanish with a flap:

The wind flung a magpie away and a black-
Back gull bent like an iron bar slowly.

The house
Rang like some fine green goblet in the note
That any second would shatter it.
Now deep
In chairs, in front of the great fire, we grip
Our hearts and cannot entertain book, thought,
Or each other.
We watch the fire blazing,
And feel the roots of the house move, but sit on,
Seeing the windows tremble to come in,
Hearing the stones cry out under the horizons.

To calm the family's nerves, Buttimer invited them into his relatively quiet front room to listen to records, but even he was spotted standing still, listening to the storm, while a needle remained upon a finished record, very uncharacteristic behaviour in one so devoted to his excellent collection of HMV 78 records!

The following evening Lucy provided another kind of drama as she brought Daisy and Elizabeth to the Gate Theatre for their first time to see *Romeo and Juliet*. Michael Mac Liammoir and Meriel Moore were in the title roles and both were superb in a lovely production. Thereafter Lucy encouraged Daisy's interest in the theatre, especially the Gate, which resulted in occasional wild dashes for last train or tram after a long performance.

It must have been heartwarming for the three sisters, Winnie, Dora and Lucy to be together again after Dora's long absence but there were certain tensions also, as one can gather from Lucy's entry: 'At "Riva" and I get several pieces of people's minds (never very complimentary) and am perturbed thereby.'

Dora and Elizabeth returned to USA where, in 1937, Dora secured a commission which added to her prestige.

This was a 'loyal address' from the members of the Washington State Branch of the English-Speaking Union. Since this tradition of presentation of addresses was unfamiliar there, but very familiar to Dora, she in fact both composed the wording and illuminated it. The occasion was the coronation of King George VI and Queen Elizabeth.

Earlier Dora had two long-term paying guests who added great interest to the household. One was a Japanese business man named Sato, and the other was the French Consul for Seattle, an elderly man as large as Sato was small. Dora was later able to use her connection with the British Consulate to obtain a position for Elizabeth on the staff, which she held for over ten years.

The phrase 'And feel the roots of the house move' quoted in relation to the storm in January proved literally true with the extreme end of Number 8 in the summer of 1936. It was found that one of the main walls was virtually unsupported, as a portion of a filled-in mine shaft under the house had subsided. This necessitated major and expensive repairs which caused great worry to Swik and Lucy and much disturbance to the tenants of the flat. Lucy described a stinking mound of earth twenty feet high in front of the flat hall door of the flat, and feared the workmen had settled down in the garden for life.

As well as the many meetings and lectures that Lucy constantly attended, she also found time to resume choral singing, as she joined the Trinity College Choral Society and enjoyed this for many years.

She was a member of the National Council of Women and would have been aware of the campaigns about the status of women in the proposed constitution of 1937, but did not take a particularly active part. However, the subject of family planning was never far from her mind and there were two quotations in her diary early in 1937. The first is from Tagore: 'This is a great movement not only because it will save women from enforced and undesirable maternity but because it will help the cause of peace by lessening the surplus population of a country scrambling for food and space outside its own rightful limits.'

She also quoted from words written by Sidney Webb: 'If a course of conduct is habitually and deliberately pursued by vast multitudes of otherwise well-conducted people forming probably a majority of the whole educated class of the nation, we must assume that it does not conflict with the actual code of morality—they are not doing what they feel to be wrong.'

Swik in his quiet way persuaded the Quakers to set up a Marriage and Parenthood Committee which lent suitable (but then banned) books to engaged couples, and arranged talks by doctors to Young Friend groups.

In 1938 Lucy attended an International Council of Women Conference in Edinburgh which was said to be the most imposing conference ever held in Scotland—'Press goes wild over us and we are principal headlines for several days. 1000 delegates from thirty-one countries—eighteen from Ireland, some of 'em bent on making trouble. In spite of that we three (Rose, self and Chenevix) enjoy ourselves and get on well together, especially enjoying the McEwan Hall Reception. The Holyrood garden party is blessed with lovely weather but is rather boring in spite of the excitement of seeing Duchess of Kent at close quarters.' (This would have been Princess Marina.)

In 1938 a new German guest was Kurt Brehmer, who had recently had to leave England after four and a half years, and had come to Ireland, but was hoping to go abroad. Lucy wrote: 'The house and garden begin to take on a new and spring-cleaned look—he paints and plasters entire greenhouse in and out, papers and paints diningroom, removes mound of earth from garden and same in front garden, converting it into a hedge in rockgarden. But more than all his labours is the spirit in which they are done—a thoroughly good influence in the house and a friend to all, even the tortoise.' He went away by bicycle after a month as Robert Burke, a cooperative farmer in Tuam, was to take him as a working guest. However, they soon heard that Kurt had been refused leave to stay in Ireland any longer. Swik went with him to the Ministry of Justice but failed to get permission to remain. Lucy wrote 'This is a disappointing ending, for there is no definite decision yet as to colonial plans. It gets on one's nerves to see the rising tide of refugees everywhere—this morning I had a letter about another case and was asked to bring it to the Jewish community.' Kurt left Ireland on 6 July and, after various vicissitudes, he was able to reach New Zealand where he settled, and in recent years became very active in supporting environmental issues.

Lucy noted in December 1938: 'These days the great appeal committee for assistance to European refugees comes out—great rage on my part and others at only one woman's name amongst fifty.'

Miss Huggard of the Coordinating Committee for Refugees asked Swik and Lucy to take Werner Schwarz (a German refugee teaching in Newtown School, Waterford) during the Christmas holiday period and he spent nearly a month with the family. He later taught fencing in Dublin and was a frequent visitor over the years.

In April 1938 all Germans then in Ireland had to vote for the *Anschluss* (annexation of Austria by Germany) on a German boat anchored at Dublin's North Wall. Not to do so would endanger permission to stay in Ireland, which was still at the discretion of the German Embassy, but Lucy commented: 'We are all sick at heart over Austria and the Spanish defeat and the advance of reaction everywhere. Better not think at all since there is nothing but "rattling back to barbarism". In September of the same year she wrote: 'The international situation goes from bad to worse. Chamberlain flies over to see Hitler and try to stay his hand—Hitler is not only trying to get entire Sudeten portion of Czechoslovakia but humiliating that country by sweeping demands, and there seems no way out of it.'

Her entry for 2–4 September 1939 was: 'Major crisis. Thunderstorm and declaration of war between England and Germany as a result of bombing of Polish towns, and floods of rain and general blackout make these few days a torment. Everyone rushes home to Ireland, crowds of people come on the boats. Ralph has his Mediterranean cruise cancelled and goes to Bangor instead. Everyone buys black material for their windows. There is a complete re-shuffle of all cabinet jobs in Ireland as in England. Now Russia takes a hand in Poland (presumably to get her whack and prevent Germany from taking too much) so we are quite hardened to shocks and surprises, and expect nothing but woes to come.'

CHAPTER EIGHTEEN
1940–1946

Lucy was very disturbed by the war, mentioning frightful raids in London and appalling damage there and in Germany. 'This war makes everything seem of no effect, importance, meaning or avail—it even vitiates the inner workings of the mind so much that it is hard to take an interest even in oneself and one's doings. All ambition that might depend on personal effort is dead, and the phrase "what's the use" or "will it be worthwhile" is always uppermost in the mind.'

In 1941 the war came closer. '1–2 January. These are bad days for Eire—bombs dropped in Borris, Drogheda, South Circular Road and Rathdown Park in Dublin—everyone mystified. Protests made to Berlin: Irish-American organisations (200) send special protest. Icy weather may be responsible for mistakes in flying direction—no one knows.' At the end of May: 'Aeroplanes roar over our heads. Awake most of the night with same, and with explosions that shake the windows—what does it all portend? Bombs dropped in North Strand, great havoc, thirty deaths or more and sixty eight injured. Awake till 4.30 with firing and aeroplanes again—utter bewilderment as to what it can mean. Frank Jones digging out for six hours on stretch'. (This was the son of their original neighbours the Joneses, who was in the St John's Ambulance Brigade). Elsa and Daisy were staying with friends in Rathfarnham and spent the night under a table, with Daisy having a vivid mental picture of Sorrento Terrace a smoking ruin!

By 1944 Lucy noted: '1. Continued successes of Russians all along west Russia and into Poland. 2. Invasion of Normandy early in June by Allies—the long-longed-for second front. 3. The coming of the V1 i.e. German invention of a pilot-less plane working havoc in Southern

England, followed in early autumn by V2, a rocket which falls without warning and travels faster than sound.'

On 25 July:'Great excitement for last two days over revolt in German Army and attempt on life of Hitler (two generals killed and one typist)—we do not know how things will shape or what effect on war as yet.'

In April 1945 Lucy noted that Germany was going from bad to worse. 'I read—for my discomfort and torture—an exposure of the extermination camps of Germany—a horrible tale.'

'May 8 1945 Peace! The news finally comes and we are knocked speechless. The International Alliance of Women gladden our hearts by getting in touch with us again and hold out hopes of a Conference in the autumn.'

Despite Lucy's account of depression at the beginning of this chapter, she had been active in many ways throughout the war years. In June 1940 she mentioned the Irish Anti-War Crusade which had been formed in 1936 and very actively run by Stanley Halliday and Betty Taylor, among others: 'Very interesting meetings these days, but pacifists are hard put to it to maintain either belief or practice in view of state of Europe with force and oppression triumphant.'

The Women's Social and Progressive League had many interesting speakers and well-attended meetings. A debate on 'Our Masculine Censorship' was so crowded that Lucy had to listen in the passage outside the room. In 1942 there was a big public meeting in the Mansion House on censorship, so it was a very live issue then.

In July 1942 Lucy got a message from Donn Piatt to say that Dr Mary Hayden was dead. She got in touch with Hanna Sheehy Skeffington and they arranged to share the press work, Lucy doing the international papers and Mrs Skeffington and the Piatts the local ones. Lucy attended the Requiem Mass and wrote: 'A great loss to feminism here as well as to scholarship.'

In August 1942 Lucy wrote: 'Go to meet those who are working to get Miss Bennett returned in Labour interest on Dun Laoghaire Borough Council—have much work in canvassing for her till 20 August , date of election. Helen Chenevix is going up for Dublin Corporation, both get in D. G., so a blow is struck for feminism, and the electorate is not entirely devoid of common sense.'

The war years brought great poverty and food shortages in Dublin. In 1941 Lucy noted: 'Robert Burke speaks on causes of war to those who are suffering from its effects. Bewley's feeding sixty children every night now and communal kitchens being talked about everywhere.' This was an emergency feeding scheme centered on Bewley's Cafes and in 1942 Lucy and Ralph gave a gramophone recital at Sorrento Terrace to raise funds for it.

In January 1944 Lucy noted: 'Rose and I to Labour Party debate on child allowances (two shillings and six pence per week for third child, if under 16!) and speak up for women having control of the allowance, such as it is.'

The following month Lucy wrote: 'My long-prepared-for address on "Feminists in Flight" takes place at Lincoln Chambers—I enjoy it greatly myself! Its preparation was certainly less of an agony than when I have to prepare a subject to order. I chose Amy Johnson and Amelia Earhart, a romantic story of their flights and aspirations, especially the latter whose explorings were as much of the mind and spirit as of the air. Very well received and I agree with the lady who sez it is the most beautiful of all addresses ever given in that room—so one has not only an appreciative audience but a self-appreciative speaker'.

In 1940 Lucy had been impressed by Father Hayes's lecture on parish councils at the Women's Progressive League. In August 1944 Lucy and Annelies went to Kilkenny for a Muintir na Tíre rural week: 'which is of great interest—fireside chats particularly, sometimes 1000 attending. Father Hayes is lovely—the moving spirit—but other priests get on my nerves. I write (with much difficulty as to sufficient leisure) a thousand-word article on my impressions and, O joyful surprise, it is printed immediately as principal article in *Irish Press*, thereby bringing me cheque for thirty-one shillings and sixpence and much satisfaction'.

The Women Citizens' Association seemed particularly active in 1944. In October Lucy noted: 'Mrs Weingreen and self have an important job for Women Citizens i.e. the giving of evidence before the Youth Unemployment Commission. Two and a half hours of ballyragging in which she, in particular, is greatly appreciated on account of knowledge of South African system of education—afterwards Dr McQuaid, Archbishop, asks her to come on the education sub-committee. One up for the good old Women Citizens.' The Citizens had also been involved in giving evidence before a Commission on Vocational Organisations, and had arranged a Conference of Social Societies to try to get some support from the medical profession on the problem of venereal disease.

In 1940 Lucy and Ralph bought an Austin which he then taught Lucy to drive. By 1941 petrol had become so scarce that it had to be laid up. Ralph and Daisy were doing volunteer work with the St John's Ambulance Brigade, Ralph doing night shifts once a week from midnight to 6 a.m. Elsa was studying music with Dina Copeman at the Royal Irish Academy of Music and obtained 94 per cent for theory.

On Christmas Day 1941, Lucy wrote: 'In the afternoon we go up to the soldiers in the park, as emissaries of the parish council and give them some gifts.' These were the small number of soldiers manning a little coast-watch station built on top of Sorrento Park. Their long boring duties were enlivened by keeping an eye on the comings and goings of 'the Terrace' directly below them. At one stage Werner Schwarz caused them great excitement by cutting his initials in the grass of the bottom lawn. This was merely to relieve the tedium of mowing the lawn but, viewed from above, looked like a signal to aircraft. Another occasion was even more serious as Werner, a keen photographer, tried to photograph the Terrace from

Bray. A German wandering round a coastal town engaged in such activities was highly suspicious and he was promptly arrested but, again with the Kingstons' assistance, was released. He had a strangely light-hearted attitude to life, especially as he was a double refugee, having had to flee first from Germany and then from Italy when Mussolini began to persecute Jews. There were at times rumours in Dalkey about the gullible Kingstons harbouring spies, but Werner would have been a liability rather than an asset to any secret organisation. The rumours were probably founded upon the fact that aliens had to report regularly to their respective embassies and, as in the case of the Austrian invasion, vote to order.

In May 1942 Lucy and Annelies cycled to Mount St Benedict near Gorey. 'A place that fires one's imagination and yet holds something of the melancholy of ancient grandeur long departed.' Father Sweetman was in charge who was a silenced priest but had run a boys' school successfully for some years and was a pioneer in growing tobacco in Ireland. The place was then run as a modestly priced guest house which Lucy greatly enjoyed visiting.

There had been an Overseas Club for some years in Dublin; its purpose was to provide social contacts for students from abroad. Through this and the Dublin International Club into which it developed in 1943, the Kingstons had entertained many Nigerian students at Sorrento Terrace. A particular friendship had developed with a Dr Sasebon and they were sorry when he returned to Lagos. He later became a well-known specialist. Lucy was interested in meeting Luba Kaftannikoff, whose poem she had quoted seventeen years previously.

Lucy had to face bereavements of increasing importance during these years. In 1940 she and Winnie were saddened by the death of Aunt Janie who had been part of their lives since childhood. She had become confused and forgetful in recent years, which had led to misunderstandings painful to Lucy. Later in the same year Tom Harrison, Liam's brother, who had shared so many musical evenings with them at Sorrento, died. Then came the sudden illness of Herbert Buttimer who was diagnosed as having diabetes with complications. He died six months later and was greatly missed, particularly by Swik. Lucy inherited his fine collection of gramophone records.

In 1943 another tragedy occurred when Ralph's inseparable friend Dell Shellard was killed by a fall from cliffs at Tramore on his twenty-fifth birthday. He was missing for four days, during which Ralph lost three-quarters of a stone weight searching for him, and he returned to Sorrento Terrace looking a wreck. Freddie Shellard, Dell's older brother, was of immense help to Ralph in coming to terms with his grief. Lucy felt the loss deeply for Ralph and also for Dell's parents, with whom she and Swik had played bridge for many years.

In 1944 there was a more cheerful note in Lucy's diary: 'Eric saves life of boy at harbour—sensation!' This was very quick action on the part of Winnie's son, aged about fourteen, who dived into the deep water at the entrance to Coliemore Harbour when he realised a young boy was in difficulties. Eric was later awarded a medal for bravery.

After the separation of the war years, Pat Butler was able to visit again in 1945 and all enjoyed the reunion. Lucy and Daisy then set off for Kylemore Abbey in Connemara, cycling from Galway, where Helen Chenevix joined them towards the end of their holiday.

On their return to Sorrento they heard that 'Milano', Vico Road, a house visible from Sorrento Terrace, was for sale. Lucy wrote: 'I fall in love with its promise of more leisured days for Swik and self—we yearn for release from the exacting and ceaseless toils of Sorrento garden, greenhouse, roof and repairs. We determine to bid at auction on Tuesday. I am at a committee when Ralph brings the news—'Milano' is ours, but at what a cost—£2330!!'

They moved on 18 October and a week later held a furniture auction. 'Not so tiring as the move, in fact great fun. Nobody could brood over old associations with such a heterogeneous swarm of hard roots in the house. Prices (particularly of rubbish) go very well and we get rid of all sorts of junk. Swik has a good deal of trouble over the legal doings and closure of sale of Number 8 Sorrento as Willie cannot come up to do this.' It was bought by the poet Francis McNamara, whose daughter Caitlin married the poet Dylan Thomas, but he was in poor health and died after a few months.

The 'old associations' referred to by Lucy above still remain in some minds, as a recent letter (July 1991) to Daisy from Frank Jones shows: 'It was a privilege to have known Mrs Kingston, more of one to have been, as I was, a frequent visitor and temporary resident in Sorrento Terrace. Your father, mother and brother were all in their separate ways very formative influences on me in my young days, and for this I am eternally grateful. In days of stultifying parochialism and repression in Ireland, they stood for independent thought and action, when neither was popular or profitable. In addition, they gave me a respect for the Society of Friends which has never left me.'

Leaving Sorrento Terrrace was a great wrench, especially for Elsa, who had been born there, and she wrote a wistful poem about it. However, Lucy found the smaller house and pocket-sized garden a great relief, but commented that Swik was far from well and was to get some leave after Christmas. Swik had been greatly tempted to retire in 1942 at age sixty, on a reduced pension. But as he and Lucy were still trying to fund Elsa's schooling and hoped to train her as a physiotherapist, and perhaps because of his increasing tendency to worry, he decided to struggle on until the age of sixty-five, despite flagging energy and increasing chest trouble.

In January Swik took sick-leave from the office and consulted his friend Dr Edward Harvey. Pleurisy was diagnosed but it then became apparent that Swik had developed the dreaded miliary tuberculosis (known as 'galloping consumption') which afflicted many younger people, but was unusual in one of his age. Lucy was so shaken that she could not even discuss it with the family, and was painfully aware that she was unsuitable as a nurse. Annelies immediately stepped into the breach and nursed this highly infectious patient to save him from having to go to hospital. With the aid of a local doctor, his suffering was alleviated as much as possible, but he died on 29 March 1946 and was buried in the Friends Burial Ground in Temple Hill, Blackrock. The day after his death Lucy wrote: 'I see him laid out and the years have dropped away, leaving him as I knew him long ago. So shall I try to remember him always, earnest for spiritual truth, keen in the use of his intellectual powers. How am I to keep the flag flying, now that I am alone?'

The family tried to emulate Lucy's stoical behaviour and must have presented an apparently calm façade, but they all suffered from their first major bereavement. The business affairs were sorted out with the help of Willie Kingston, and it was generously indicated that Elsa's proposed training could continue, with Quaker grants for her fees. Lucy received only the equivalent of one and a half year's salary, as there were no widows' pensions for civil servants then. She had, however, a small income from investments as well as modest household contributions from Ralph and Daisy.

Lucy took a very positive step to assuage her profound feeling of loss. She gathered up Swik's many essays and religious and philosophical musings and went to the haven of Mount St Benedict again. There, in the undisturbed calm of the place she knew well, she assembled a booklet of poems and essays by Swik which she called *Remnants of Faith*. This she had privately printed. Copies were distributed among Quakers, who had appreciated his utterances over the years, when he had been a valued member of the Society, and to many of his other friends. It was a therapeutic undertaking and she returned to 'Milano' and her normal activities, with Annelies living with the family between her nursing cases.

CHAPTER NINETEEN
1947–1956

During the years 1947 to 1954 the world was trying to recover from the war. Annelies Becker undertook work with Friends Relief Service in Germany and later in Vienna, under the auspices of the American Friends' Service Committee.

The growth of nuclear armaments greatly concerned Lucy and in March 1954 she commented: 'Frightful world outlook: hydrogen bomb insanity reaching a peak.' She joined in the sending of protests about bomb tests in various parts of the world. She was one of a deputation of Quakers to see Sean MacBride, then Minister of External Affairs. 'Well received, we find him charming, natural, pleasant and internationally-minded but nevertheless a trifle sad. He agrees with all, and urges us in addition to work for abolition of capital punishment: and to consult him at will, while he is in office.'

In June 1948 Lucy gave a small tea-party to 'the remnant of Women Citizens who are now officially the international sub-committee of the Irish Housewives' Association, but are otherwise unchanged'. At a later crowded general meeting of the Housewives, she noted: 'Dr Noel Browne speaks and is very inspiring in his young enthusiasm'. In November she was requested to write an article on the history of the Irish Women Citizens' Association but found that all papers had been destroyed and had to rely on her memory (or even her imagination) for the *Irish Housewives' Annual*.

A World Pacifist Meeting was being planned when Gandhi was assassinated in January 1948. Despite this shocking event, pacifists worldwide were anxious to further his work. They arranged to hold the meeting at the end of 1949, based at Santiniketan, the home of the late poet Tagore, and at Sevagram, one of Gandhi's ashrams. Lucy was delighted when she was offered a place, especially as she had been so deeply interested in Indian affairs since 1930. Travelling by sea in the cheapest way, she and the other delegates from thirty-five countries attended the conference, meeting Pandit Nehru and Dr Prasad. They then travelled to other parts of India, staying at Indian homes and visiting hospitals, ashrams and educational institutions, and being garlanded at every opportunity, as is the charming Indian custom.

Lucy was away for three months, returning in January 1950, when she spoke on her experiences to the Women's Progressive League and to other groups. Lucy was chairperson of the League and Rose was honorary secretary during 1949–50 and there were eighty-three paid-up members.

1949 brought many changes within the family. In January Ralph became engaged to Dorothy Tracey and Daisy to William Swanton. William (as Lucy always insisted on calling him, though he was known universally as Bill) and Daisy had the complications of requiring a dispensation from Rome (Daisy being an unbaptised person) and she had to take instruction before it would be granted. There were many rules and regulations relating to the wedding in those very rigid times. As Dorothy was a member of the Church of Ireland, her and Ralph's arrangements were simpler, and both couples planned June weddings. All through the years Lucy and Winnie had kept contact, frequently arguing and disagreeing, but both rather enjoyed sparring with one another. Now, however, their disagreements became very painful over Winnie's attitude to mixed marriage and Lucy wrote: 'Winnie still on the rampage and refuses to meet W. Swanton. Vitriolic and sporadic letters'.

Ralph and Dorothy agreed to take over 'Milano', and Lucy joined with Rose in renting the upper half of 17 Charleville Road, Rathmines, overlooking the St Louis

Convent grounds. Rose's main requirement was easy access for her cat and this was assured by a shed-roof adjoining Rose's bedroom window. Neither she nor Lucy was domesticated or keen on cooking, so they shared a tiny kitchenette without friction, each providing her own meals, as Rose was a vegetarian. They had a bedroom and a sitting room each. Given their long friendship and shared interests, it was an ideal arrangement. Meanwhile, William and Daisy had taken a small flat about half a mile away. Elsa passed her physiotherapy examination and obtained a position in Newtownards, County Down, so was only an occasional visitor from then on.

An enterprising action taken by Lucy, in view of her widowed state and Elsa's departure, was to reply to an advertisement from a middle-aged widow seeking companionship. This was a northside Dubliner with whom she formed a pleasant relationship, especially for occasional holidays and theatre and cinema outings. Though her friend was not committed to causes in any way, they both enjoyed their contacts for many years.

The Swantons moved to a flat in Number 15 Charleville Road towards the end of 1950, thus continuing the old family habit of living close to mother. About six months later, the lower flat in Number 17 became vacant so they moved in, Rose continuing to be calmly welcoming to this family encroachment.

In 1950 the news from Seattle was that Elizabeth was being moved to Quito, in Ecuador, to the distress of her parents. Elizabeth spent two years in Ecuador and was then posted to the Foreign Office in London. In Quito she had met a botanist, Peter Bell, and found he was returning to London on the same ship. She was a second-class passenger and he a third, and the ship rules were that 'never the twain should meet'! However, Peter made sure he circumvented the rules and they were soon engaged.

Liam's health had been giving anxiety, as he had developed angina, so in 1951 he and Dora decided to return to Ireland, and obtained a flat in Derrymore, with the same aspect as 'Riva', and only a few minutes walk from Winnie's new house 'Gwyndy' at Coliemore Harbour, Dalkey.

Lucy's first grandchild, Sylvia Helene Swanton, was born in October 1951. In 1952 there were again two weddings within a month, as Elsa married Gray Peile and Elizabeth married Peter Bell.

Lucy took up a part-time position as librarian in the Friends' Library in Eustace Street, which she enjoyed. This also led to her dealing with correspondence from enquirers about Quakerism and interviewing them, if they so wished.

When Annelies returned from Vienna, she undertook a Social Science diploma course in Trinity College and then did social work in London, so she returned to stay with Lucy only occasionally.

Lucy was not neglecting her reading and had copied many quotations from Evelyn Underhill, Arnold Bennett and this from George Eliot: 'In many of our neighbours' lives there is much not only of error and lapse but of a certain exquisite goodness which can never be written or even spoken—only divined by each of us, according to the inward instruction of our own privacy.' (*Daniel Deronda*)

As she got older, Lucy seemed to develop this capacity and it made her very sensitive in relating to people. She was also capable of feeling deep impatience with those who disagreed with her, especially on committees! Because of her espousal of liberal issues, she was viewed with suspicion by some who feared she leaned to the left, as communism was the great bogey of the 1950s.

Lucy enjoyed many meetings of the Contemporary Club and in November 1953 noted: 'Meeting is addressed by Donal Nevin, a clever young economist, on partition and unemployment—much speaking, in which I in foolhardy mood introduce the subject of family planning as it is begun in India'. She had during that year been accepted as a subscribing member of the International Planned Parenthood Association. She was not clear as to how an isolated member could be of much use, but was cheered to hear (through *International Women's News*) of their existence and activities. An added pleasure to Lucy was that their paper came regularly to her in a plain brown wrapper, thus breaking censorship regulations which were still strictly applied in the Fifties.

Lucy acquired two more granddaughters: Karin Lucy Peile was born in August 1953 and Diane Lawrenson Kingston in March 1954. Dora had also become a grandmother with the birth of Michael Geoffrey Harrison Bell in October 1953.

In May 1954 Lucy was pained by the sad, but not unexpected, death of Francie Jones 'one of our longest-standing family friends', and later was grieved to hear of the death of Mrs Shellard.

In June Lucy was alarmed to hear of Ralph having had an emergency operation for kidney stones when on holiday with Dorothy in the Isle of Man. He suffered severe post-operational shock and did not return until July looking 'old and emaciated'.

In August Lucy wrote: 'I go to 'Milano' for tea and see Diane looking strong and contented, Ralph looking better, and go with him to the meeting of Dalkey Protesters re Vico Road building—crowded to doors and many outside. Very masculinist platform, only Mrs Garrioch representing the women of Dalkey. I propose her for the Vico Road committee nominated by the meeting.' Mrs Garrioch was a near neighbour of the Budds and her sons had grown up with Ralph. This Vico Road row was occasioned by a house having been built which obscured the view, and by public protest the builders were forced to lower the roof. The Kingstons were very concerned about this, as years before Swik had acted with a group of other residents to ensure that Vico Road would not have buildings on the sea side, so as to preserve the amenities for all citizens.

In February 1955 Lucy noted that the Women's Progressive League were cooperating with the Irish

Housewives' Association in hosting a visit to Dublin of Madame Vijaya Lakshmi Pandit, Indian Ambassador to Ireland, but based in London. On 4 March Lucy wrote: 'This afternoon is the big event for Madame Pandit in Hibernian Hotel, 170 talking women. Mrs Dixon introduces speaker shortly and after her equally short speech we sit to the meal. Find her less formidable, in fact quite approachable: wonder about possibility of getting her to intercede with Minister for External Affairs re financing congress work.'

In October Lucy attended a meeting on cooperation at the Irish Women Workers' Union and found herself beside Mrs Marie Johnson: 'whom I have not spoken to for at least twenty five years, and we renew acquaintance—one of the few old suffragettes and WIL members left.'

In April 1956 Lucy noted: 'Tonight a memorable meeting on tolerance at Contemporary Club, Patrick Ward, a young orthodox Catholic speaking to the subject. Owen Sheehy Skeffington, Gore-Grimes and many another worry him like a rat—I also give a few bites but must admire his good-natured reaction to all this.'

In July 1956 Lucy and Rose went to a WILPF Conference in Birmingham where Lucy again met Gertrud Baer, whom she had first met in 1926.

There were many happenings in her personal life during these years. First, she was very depressed to hear that Dora and Liam planned to move from Dalkey to London to be nearer Elizabeth. In May Lucy attended the Prizewinners' Concert of the Feis Ceoil with Dora and had 'a heavenly time with a wonderful standard of performance'. Then she said farewell to them in June. In July she went to a small garden party at Ruby Holt's where she met Michael and Grainne Yeats and their three children: 'I dandle in my arms the three-month old granddaughter of the poet Yeats and think how queer life is'.

On 21 October 1955 Lucy wrote: 'Natal day of first grandson Richard Samuel Swanton (after two grandfathers) 7 lbs 5 oz and a touching little specimen, half tortoise and half mole.' Ten days later Brian Leslie arrived, born to Ralph and Dorothy: 'but a small minority think that Daisy has had twins!'. In May 1956 Elsa followed suit by producing Lawrence Gray Peile, the third grandson for Lucy.

In March 1955 Ralph and Dorothy bought a house called 'Arcot' in Blackrock so Lucy had to relet 'Milano'.

The Peiles and Swantons left for a combined holiday in the West of Ireland in August 1956 and on 7 August Lucy went to have tea with Ralph and Dorothy and see her grandchildren Diane and Brian. On 9 August Lucy was rung after midnight by Dorothy's mother: 'with shocking news which I can't absorb about Ralph's "heart attack". Go out to 'Arcot' and find house crowded with people, including two guards who later question me but not Dorothy, who is in a sorry state. Ralph taken away by doctor to Monkstown Hospital before I get there.' Gradually Lucy pieced together the awful reality which was that Ralph had accidentally killed himself trying to ease another asthma attack by taking a whiff of chloroform. He had made up an elaborate mask to protect his face from the fumes, but had been overcome before he realised the danger. Later Dorothy showed Lucy a book in which this had been suggested as a possible ease for an asthma spasm, but she knew nothing of his wish to experiment.

Lucy wired to Daisy and Elsa, who returned from Newport at once, and Willie Kingston also came immediately. The funeral took place at Temple Hill with a very large attendance of stricken young men, as Ralph had many contacts through his work and dance bands. The family attended the inquest when Lucy noted: 'Coroner vacillated over the word "accidental" or "probably accidental" in a harrassing way; glad it is over at last but not quite prepared for the unwanted reports in six papers.'

There was incessant rain and thunder for the rest of the month but at the beginning of September Lucy noted: 'At last there seems a let-up of this dismal dreary rain which has so accentuated the troubles of this last ghastly month, now happily over. Still hard to get rid of this feeling of utter unreality. On 15 September rain again descends on us, and what with that and all else, reach a new low in depression. I feel like an old piano that can carry on with its music but has a jangling wire within that never stops.' The loss of a sensitive, helpful and humorous son only thirty-eight years old was a calamity that took all Lucy's courage to endure during the ensuing years. She went to London to Dora and Liam, glad to be diverted for a while by new scenes. She returned on 1 October feeling renewed and ready to cope once more, and bravely resumed her normal activities, but during October she copied out a poem by Walter de la Mare, adding a significant date to the title:

Autumn
(9 August 1956)
There is wind where the rose was;
Cold rain where sweet grass was;
And clouds like sheep
Stream o'er the steep
Grey skies where the lark was.

Nought gold where your hair was;
Nought warm where your hand was;
But phantom, forlorn,
Beneath the thorn,
Your ghost where your face was.

Sad winds where your voice was;
Tears, tears where my heart was;
And ever with me,
Child, ever with me,
Silence where hope was.

CHAPTER TWENTY
1956–1959

In November 1956 Lucy was: 'Fighting with recurrent depression which however on all accounts might be even worse,' Then came the news of Louie Bennett's death: 'Another gallant soul moves into the silent land.' Lucy attended the funeral where she noted that Helen Chenevix looked stricken.

There had been a much publicised case of a trial of Nurse Cadden for carrying out an abortion with the consequent death of the patient. Lucy was shocked when the judge gave the death sentence, stating that the motive did not matter, even if the 'victim' was in agreement. It seemed to Lucy utterly barbaric not to give a verdict of manslaughter in such circumstances. She brought the matter to the Quaker meeting in Dublin which issued a statement against capital punishment. The death sentence was subsequently commuted to penal servitude for life, but after a year Nurse Cadden was transferred to the Criminal Mental Hospital in Dundrum where she died a year later.

This whole problem of abortion must have remained in Lucy's mind, as in 1961 she had in her journal a quotation from herself as follows:

'We condone and have always condoned war since earliest Christian times—but we will not condone nor encourage the death of a foetus. How is it not more immoral and more heartless to bring about (through war) the slaughter of a fully grown young man, to the desolation and spiritual agony of his loved ones, and the physical agony of himself—than it is to extinguish painlessly a life that has yet no consciousness nor feeling, or even to prevent its coming, considering that too-abundant life is the increasing problem of this age and itself a cause of wars, as well as of many attendant evils. ' (Self, June '61 but oh! how unavailing!)

In early December 1956 Lucy had to go out to Dalkey in connection with repairs to 'Milano'. She visited Winnie and heard that Elizabeth had had a second son Jeremy and that all was well. Lucy added: 'Dalkey looks very enchanting, with young crescent moon and fine clear night. How did we not expire with ecstasy in those past years amidst such scenery, and before all these troubles came on us?'

Before Ralph's death Lucy had been vaguely house-hunting as they needed more room with the Swantons' growing family, and Lucy's and Rose's hospitable instincts. After viewing various large old houses which all proved far too expensive, she discovered Wynnefield House at the cul-de-sac end of Charleville Road. It was a three-storey Georgian house adjoining the St Louis Convent, with some fine old trees, a large back garden, a rockery, long lawn and small greenhouse, giving space and privacy—yet it was only two miles from the GPO. Lucy agreed to take on the remainder of a repairing lease from the lessees for £650. and Rose and the Swantons were her tenants, all sharing the telephone and electricity bills. They moved there on 28 February 1957, this being the third house in the same road occupied by the Swantons!

Lucy was surprised to hear that five people wanted to suggest her name as a Housewives' Candidate in the forthcoming general election: 'Can hardly take this seriously.' On 13 February she went to 'a tempestuous meeting of Housewives (standing throughout as is now usual with latecomers). Four names, including mine, put up as election candidates but I withdraw, leaving Mrs McGuinness, Mrs Dixon and Miss Kathleen Swanton.' Rose and Lucy then canvassed for Mrs Dixon in the Rathmines constituency, but she was not elected. A detailed and interesting account of this election campaign is in the published story of the IHA , *A Link in the Chain* by Hilda Tweedy.

In May 1957 Lucy was considerably shaken to hear that Dorothy was contemplating marrying Jim Murray, whom she had known in the past and who lived in Larne. Lucy had been trying to keep in touch with Ralph's children, having a special feeling for Diane who looked so like Ralph did when he was a baby, and contact would be very much harder to keep up if and when they moved to Larne. Dorothy married Jim in September and later Lucy quoted: 'Grass grows over every grave, but there are some deaths that reduce the survivors for ever to a lower level of happiness'—adding that such words seemed to speak of the family's depression at that time.

During 1958 there was much publicity about the Campaign for Nuclear Disarmament in Britain. On 25 April Lucy and Daisy held a meeting at 'Wynnefield' to hear Conor Farrington's account of the H-Bomb March in London. Lucy noted: 'Another committee is formed (perhaps ad hoc) to pursue the matter and bring in others.' This is one of the earliest references to Irish CND. Lucy noted about twenty-seven present and much enthusiasm. In March 1959 Lucy was elected to the CND Council with sixteen others, but resisted appointment to the executive committee.

In September 1958 Lucy was present when a Louie Bennett Memorial Seat was unveiled by Mrs Byrne, Lord Mayor, in St. Stephen's Green. Helen Chenevix spoke and then John Swift. It was a fine morning and there were about one hundred people present, many of whom were known to Rose and Lucy.

During 1958 Lucy acquired two further grand-daughters, Elaine Charlotte Peile in May and Eva Olive Swanton in December. Lucy was very interested in the developing character of Sylvia, her eldest granddaughter, and felt that her remark when about to make her First Communion: 'I don't think Gran would like to give me the veil' was one that in its insight should go down to posterity. The house was humming with activity and, in Rose's phrase, 'the thunder of little feet'. Lucy wrote of one night when there were three concurrent committees, one in her room, one in Daisy's, and an anti-vivisection conclave in Rose's room.

Daisy had engaged a French *au pair* for the summer months of 1959 and Lucy wrote: 'Look out on a sunny scene from my drawingroom window—one should catch the moment, I suppose. The French girl dandles Eva in the bright July warmth, dance-music sounds in the background; the roses sway in the breeze. Richard, like a fairer and more sophisticated edition of little Lord Fauntleroy, rolls his coaster around, looking up for praise or at least admiring glances. O, Ralph, why are you not here to see, why did you leave us—I am often so resigned to your going from this vale of tears—but not always, not on a day like this.'

Early in December Rose was told that Tom Jacob had had a serious attack of coronary thrombosis and then Lucy wrote: 'Louis comes with news that Tom, the beloved Tom, passed away this afternoon—only a week since he was here to tea with Rose and self. Something is gone out of Rose's life—quite irreplaceable.'

CHAPTER TWENTY-ONE
1960–1969

The 1960s were times of great tension internationally. In 1961 Lucy wrote: 'News very grave, Kennedy provocative to dangerous degree and called up millions more men for military training. Kruschev convulsed with rage'. Later in August she noted 'All very anxious over the seeming impasse between Russia and United Nations over East Berlin—Earl Russell makes startling appeals for sanity, grand man, may he live long—and indeed he has!'

In September 1961 she wrote: 'Everyone horrified by international news. Kruschev to re-start nuclear tests—every day brings news of a fresh one tried—in Central Asia, in Arctic—what does it mean?'

In October Lucy went to a Housewives meeting on the Common Market 'addressed by a very brilliant young woman called Hederman—an enthusiast on (even) such an uninspiring subject.'

As well as her work on the Council of Irish CND, Lucy gave much support to the Irish Pacifist Movement who were very active then. She and Daisy hosted a fund-raising anti-nuclear fête and bring-and-buy Sale at 'Wynnefield' in September 1960 of which Lucy recounted: 'A day of blazing sunshine in this awful month—and badly needed! Our fête proceeds with unexpected brilliance and success—decorations, balloons, music, drinks (soft) and much bunting, plus two ponies, hosts of children, photos for *Press* (not always appearing) and the *Independent*, and a photographer who had as his last photograph Kruschev (out East at some Conference!). Dr J. de Courcy Ireland orates from the steps, quite suitably to his audience, and Ciaran MacAnally and Stanley Halliday release gas-filled balloons and later word was received that one had reached Scotland.'

Lucy had to face another bereavement shortly after this event. On 24 September she and Rose attended the Ideal Homes Exhibition at the Mansion House for four hours trying to interest people in *The Irish Housewife* magazine, and encouraging them to join the association. The next day Lucy wrote: 'Alas, poor Rose. On way to Harold's Cross Hospice, she is run down by car, legs broken, head injured and doctor fears pelvis also broken—I go down about 2 o'clock after guards visit to tell us.' On 11 October Lucy was informed that Rose had died early that morning. 'Goodbye, old and long-standing companion—I should have been more patient had I known you were going to slip away like this. Three guards come to get information for inquest, and seem to have it in mind to make manslaughter charge against the young man who did this thing—I do hope they will do nothing of the kind: he has suffered enough and moreover seems to have two witnesses in his favour.' (He was later acquitted). 'Fuss about where the remains will be buried so we offer room in Temple Hill plot to save journey to Waterford. Funeral at 2.30 on 13 October. Very large number, a "representative" funeral, but so many things to represent! The nationalist side seen to by Dev. who sends emissary, and some Friends—not used to such a proceeding—pretend to fear he may fire a volley over the grave!' Rose was buried in a plot beside the graves of Swik and Ralph.

Lucy stuck into her journal an anonymous printed verse which seemed extremely apt:

I did not know that you were old until you died;
I thought that you were young—so great your great
    soul's pride
Then I remembered all—your sometime slowing
    pace,
Your shoulder's little stoop, the look withdrawn
    upon your tranquil face.
I did not know that you were old until you died;
    Then I perceived.

For the next few months Margie Shanahan visited frequently to clear and sort her aunt's belongings. She and her children had attended the large combined children's birthday parties, another of which was held this year, as Lucy still felt that 'mourning would mar and maim', as in the 'Burial' poem previously mentioned.

In March 1961 Liam died in London and Lucy felt very concerned about Dora's mental confusion.

1961 brought Lucy much involvement with the Housewives, particularly the international side of their work, as they were to host an International Alliance of Women's Congress in Dublin. In March Lucy wrote: 'Go to IHA meeting and it is well I did so, as there is a row over my being a "delegate" and I am suggested to be put on a list of "provisionals"—which rouses two heroines and they retire in my favour—two others have also, I hear, threatened to resign as secretaries. All this creates wonder in my bosom and I feel like someone in a lonely grave who suddenly has suicides taking place for her dear sake. Wonders will never cease—but am I right to accept a place as a delegate?'

These difficulties within the Housewives were intensifying as the more liberal members were being viewed with suspicion and distrust. Again in June Lucy wrote 'At highly irritating meeting of "the delegates" (twelve in number attending) about Congress plans and working programme. Very retrogressive atmosphere on many questions, including school meals, nursery centres etc. I never miss Rose so greatly as on these occasions, she never let anything in the nature of a backwash towards anti-feminism pass without protest. Wish there were more "protestants" in this sense. Much cast down'. On 27 June: 'Go to General Committee of Housewives and hear Andrée Sheehy Skeffington has been refused an invitation to Congress and Miss Blake has been called a Communist—Mrs Sawier tells me more when coming home, a frightful set.' Later Helen Chenevix and Lucy protested by letter about Andrée Sheehy Skeffington and did not get a satisfactory answer. These were the years when Owen Sheehy Skeffington was fighting (often a lone voice) in the Seanad and in public life for liberal issues, frequently being banned from addressing meetings. This may have been the reason for this baffling distrust of Andrée. She had been a founder member of the IHA and a very active joint secretary with Hilda Tweedy in the early years of the Association.

Another possible reason for the uneasiness some IHA members felt about Lucy was her long years of association with Rose Jacob, who was always an outspoken humanist in her views. Rose had been brought up by strongly humanist parents who had resigned from the Quakers in Waterford. Rose's friendship with Miss Blake and others of similar views were upsetting to the increasingly conventional tendency within the IHA.

Finally on 21 August the congress opened and lasted a fortnight. 'Endless meetings, committees, a few wrangles and misunderstandings. I dodge the night engagements, also the excursions, too busy. Helen Chenevix stays the course wonderfully well. I have seventeen to tea to meet the two nice WILPF observers, Mrs Stapleton and Dr Elsa Zeuther (Denmark). We agree to have a correspondent, if not a Branch, of WIL and Dr Rose Heitler is to be that person. They leave about seven, a good job done.' This appeared to be the end of Lucy's involvement with the international side of the Housewives.

In 1962 Lucy noted a big AGM of the Irish Pacifist Movement: 'New chairman is now Brian Boydell, Vice-presidents are Helen Chenevix, Eoin O'Mahony and Ciaran MacAnally, who gives long and very interesting address on the Catholic Conference held at Spode House, Staffordshire.'

In September 1962 Lucy travelled to London with Betty de Courcy Ireland to a European Federation Conference of CND. 'Fourteen men and four women at Congress.

German is spoken mainly with varying accents, but all know some English. I lift up my voice and speak of Ireland at public meeting in Church House, St Paul's. Canon Collins chairs the group meetings.'

In March 1962 Lucy's ninth and last grandchild Owen Kingston Peile was born in Portadown. Lucy's comment was: 'Am greatly pleased with sight of Owen Kingston, a nicely coloured small neat object, expression full of dignity and conscientiousness!' Throughout the years of being a grandmother, Lucy had been a great support to Elsa, who frequently contracted influenza and needed help. Daisy had recurrent bouts of asthma and Lucy assisted her in many ways, not least in encouraging the children to read. Lucy was charmed to find she had inculcated a love of books in Eva who, at the age of two and a quarter, asked Lucy to 'bring a book from Lib-ee'.

Dora left London and settled briefly in a flat in Dun Laoghaire. As she was becoming vague and forgetful, Mrs Ashmore kindly offered a very small flat in 'Derrymore' so Dora returned there to more sheltered accommodation. By a coincidence, Theodora FitzGibbon had a flat in the house also, and there was much confusion over post, Dora naturally assuming that anything on which she saw 'Theodora' was her property. In January 1963 Lucy wrote: 'During the following four weeks weather is dramatically severe all over Europe, and other places—we have severest frost conditions recorded for 200 years, surpassing the severities of 1947. Killarney Lakes frozen— sea frozen in places, widespread damage.'

Lucy was reading *To Katanga and Back* by Conor Cruise O'Brien and rereading *Under the Net* by Iris Murdoch—'a capital and unique book'.

In April Brenda Yasin, secretary of the Irish Pacifist Movement, and Mrs Robertson paid a visit to Pope John XXIII re his peace asserverations and appeals. Lucy went to meet them at the airport on their return, but regretted that there was not as much attention from the press as their cause deserved. She had copied extracts from the Pope's encyclical letter *Pacem in Terris* into her journal. Later she noted his illness and death 'one whom we as pacifists must and do lament'.

On 23 November 1963 she wrote: 'Assassination of President Kennedy. A miserable day not unlike January 1948 when Gandhi was shot. We cancel the motorcade planned by CND but some of us foregather at Merrion Square and a few go on to French Embassy with letter re French tests. The Ambassador received this small delegation and "explained" French policy.'

Lucy had to face another personal loss during this year. She had known that Helen Chenevix was very ill in Monkstown Hospital and, being told of her death on 4 March, wrote 'Very depressed, who can ever take her place?' She attended the funeral at Deansgrange, referring to the excellent tribute paid by Rory Roberts. She then wrote a short appreciation for *Peace News* and for *Pax et Libertas*, the WILPF journal. 'Farewell, another friend.'

In June 1964 another long-standing friend, Ruby Holt, died. Lucy attended the funeral and was very depressed: 'so I go forth and have a set of coloured photographs taken (with the thought in mind "while the going is good")'. Lucy was still working in the Friends Library but found it rather desolate and depressing, part of her general depression after Ruby's death.

During this year a notorious murder case greatly concerned Lucy. A young South African Indian medical student/chef had murdered his Irish fiancée in a fit of jealousy and had then, panic-stricken, dismembered her body, in the hope of hiding it among the refuse from the restaurant. The brutality of the accounts shocked Lucy, but she was also shocked by the death penalty being passed upon the young man, especially as the girl's family had been outstandingly forgiving. Lucy tried to stir up the Civil Liberties Association to protest about the death penalty and plead for mercy, and also raised the matter among Dublin Quakers. They agreed that a letter of sympathetic concern should be written to Shan Mohangi's mother in Natal and this was composed by Lucy and Victor Bewley. They were pleased to receive a reply. The death sentence was commuted to life imprisonment and Mohangi was released after ten years and became a public representative in South Africa later on.

An ambitious venture was undertaken in 1966 with a group of Fellowship of Reconciliation members from England, Scotland and Ireland. This was a ten-day coach tour through Belgium, West and East Germany and Czechoslovakia. Elsa accompanied Lucy and realized that her mother's memory was beginning to fail in much the same way that Dora's had. A report of this tour among Lucy's papers ends with the words: 'The fact that we were on a goodwill journey was appreciated by those we met, and though it may be only a drop in the ocean, in the words of a Berlin Friend: 'What ocean is not made up of tiny drops?'

In 1967 Winnie's health started to be cause for concern and in April she died after a short illness, tenderly cared for by Robin, who continued to live in Dalkey and kept in touch with the family.

Lucy's last public service meant a great deal to her. Partly on her initiative, a committee had been formed to add a plaque to the Louie Bennett seat, commemorating Helen Chenevix's life. A rather touching *Irish Times* photograph shows Sybil Le Brocquy, who unveiled the plaque, with Lucy and the then very aged Marie Johnson. Lucy's note was: '16 November. Unveiling over at last, great success—Mrs Le Brocquy does the preliminary speech, good attendance, Mrs Johnson still extant, all committee except the two authors attend [Peadar O'Donnell and R. M. Fox]. *Irish Times* acted correctly throughout—as everyone did, except the Irish Women Workers' Union whose defection remains a complete mystery.'

Daisy then had the unenviable task of telling Lucy that William proposed taking early retirement and moving to Cobh. He warmly urged Lucy to move with them, but she would not contemplate this, as Dublin life meant so much to her. She enquired about the Quaker Retirement Home at Swanbrook, off Morehampton Road, and was fortunate to secure a room. In 1967 Dora's mental confusion had become so marked that Elizabeth found a place for her in Bloomfield Hospital, beside Swanbrook. It is strange to see the family pattern of living near together repeated for Dora's last six months, as she died peacefully in July 1969, shortly after her seventy-ninth birthday. Lucy had not been able to have much contact with her since she was admitted to Bloomfield Hospital, but it was a very sad time for her nevertheless. In February 1969 Daisy and Eva brought Lucy to Swanbrook, where she had a pleasant room which accommodated her piano and some of her furniture. The Swantons did not finally move to Cobh until July, so Lucy and Daisy were able to phase out their long companionship, but neither found it easy.

In November 1969 Lucy became ill at Swanbrook and was moved to St Vincent's Hospital. She asked Daisy to find her 'somewhere with peace and quiet' (Swanbrook was not able to cope with invalids) and on 10 December Daisy took Lucy out to Dr Eustace's Home at Hampstead in Glasnevin, where Lucy had visited her old friend Miss Eustace long ago. On 18 December Lucy had a second stroke and developed pneumonia. She died at 2.20 a.m. on 23 December. Funeral arrangements had to be made hurriedly, in view of the long Christmas break, so Lucy was buried at Temple Hill on 24 December. As this was Christmas Eve, very few people would have noted the death announcement, and therefore Daisy and Elsa were very touched by the presence of an unexpected mourner. As they approached the little Meeting House and saw the usual groups of Quakers, a tall figure greeted them whom Daisy knew to be Fred Johnson. He had been asked by his

mother Marie to represent her, and Daisy realised how
deeply pleased Lucy would have been at this link with
one of her earliest contacts with feminism and the
beginning of the Women's International League.

Song

I said, 'The World will all be gay when the summer
    comes,
When the summer comes,
These grieving hours will pass away
And warmth and glory fill each day when the
    glorious summer comes.'
The summer came; but the heavy rains
Came too, and now the season wanes,
But my shadow still remains.

I said: 'Maturity will come; it will gladden me it will
    brighter be,
And Truth will make my heart its home and will set
    my nature free.
Happy and free my thought shall roam.'
But I grew in years and my pain still grew,
And I brooded oft and I sighed oft too,
And the cause I never knew.

'But Love will come,' again I said,
'With his conqu'ring power, with his glorious
    power'.
He came one day and his radiance shed
A joy o'er every hour.
But he played me false and my love lay dead.
Then the skies were dark and the night-wind's
    moan
Was sad to me; for to me was known,
This grief,—to be alone.

I said, 'No longer will I pine,

For my summer day for my hour sublime,
It comes to all, and it will be mine
If I wait the gods' good time
Where beyond earth's dreaming hopes will shine
A land of Truth, not a pit of pain.
When I shall know and be known again
Can the shadow there remain?
L. O. K.

SELECT BIBLIOGRAPHY

Brockie, Gerard and Raymond Walsh. *Focus on the Past 3.* Dublin: Gill and Macmillan, 1991.

Casserley, H. C. *Outline of Irish Railway History.* Devon: David and Charles Publishers, 1974.

Harrison, Richard S. *Irish Anti-War Movements 1824-1974.* Dublin: Irish Peace Publications, 1986.

McCay, Hedley. *Padraic Pearse.* Cork: Mercier Press, 1966.

Missing Pieces, Women in Irish History, 1: Since the Famine. Dublin: Irish Feminist Information Publications Ltd, 1983.

More Missing Pieces. Dublin: Attic Press, 1985.

Murphy, John A., *Ireland in the Twentieth Century.* Dublin: Gill and Macmillan, 1989.

Owens, Rosemary Cullen. *Smashing Times.* Dublin: Attic Press, 1984.

Sheehy Skeffington, Andrée; *Skeff.* Dublin: Lilliput Press, 1991.

Tweedy, Hilda. *A Link in the Chain.* Dublin: Attic Press, 1992.

Wagner, Gillian. *Barnardo.* London: Wiedenfeld and Nicholson, 1979.

Ward, Margaret. *The Missing Sex.* Dublin: Attic Press, 1991.

INDEX